CULTURE AND COLLECTIONS

CULTURE AND COLLECTIONS

Humanistic amalgam of Tantra, Vaisnavism, Saivism and Folkcults

EDITOR

DR. RAMPRASAD MISHRA

Contributors

DR. U. N. MAHANTY

DR. D. BISHI

PUNTHI-PUSTAK

CALCUTTA : : 1996

Published By :

S. K. BHATTACHARYA
PUNTHI-PUSTAK
Publishers, Booksellers & Exporter,
136/4B, Bidhan Sarani,
P. O. Box No : 16602
Calcutta-700 004. (INDIA)

First Published 1996

ISBN : 81-85094-99-3

Rs. 250.00

Printed at :
Bilash Hazra
Modern Printers
61/B, Shyampukur Street,
Calcutta-700 004.

DEDICATION

"Saṁsārārṇava Karṇadhāramapitam Bhaktārtha Saṁsāriṇaṁ
Vande Śrī Puruṣottama tanubhṛitām Saṁkalpa Kalpadrumaṁ
Vedāntārthamudāharanti Khalu Yaṁ Yenākhilaṁ bhāsate
hriste yatra hṛiṇiyate Padamapi Svāyambhuvaṁ dehināṁ".

Dedicated at the lotus-feet of Lord Jagannāth, the presiding Lord of the Cosmos Who appears as Buddha to the Buddhists, Jīna to the jainas, Viṣṇu to the Vaiṣṇavas, Śiva to the Śaivas, Śakti to the Śāktas, Sūrya to the Sauras, Gaṇapati to the Gāṇapatyas, Āllāh to the Muslims, Supreme Lord and Universal Father to the Christians and the Grand Synthesis of all divinities in India and abroad.

Editor

CONTENTS

EDITORIAL

EDITORIAL

Culture, while presenting a wider connotation through the prolific pens of many eminent and erudite authors of the world has really been considered as a large index of the benefic contour of human civilisation. It is indeed a finer achievement of man for the benefit of man in the society. Encompassing from ages together the thought, action, genius, creativity and the living-philosophy of man it has inspired its creaters in various dynamic aspects to bring out the real identity of man, the best creature of the animate world for the benefit of themselves as also for that of others in a simultaneous trend. The real identity of man, the best and the rational among the animal world lies in his cognition and creativity for the betterment of himself and the world-order around and is not confined to the building of his career, fortune and his standard of living even in term of a narrow individual happiness or a mutually comfortable co-existence of narrower area. It really denotes his aspiration and activity for building Humanism, the surest safeguard for the piously cherished perennial continuity of the world-order.

Religion subscribes a lion's share to the evolution of culture especially in its doctrine and development of its morality and service. While embodying various beliefs and practices for its institutional development in the human society it aims at the moral upliftment of all its real followers and inspires them to identify the vitality of individual creature as one and the same among these of others. It speculates every individual vitality as a part of the cosmic vital energy to which it calls as Almighty God, parameśvara, Āllāh, supreme reality Parambrahman, Paramātman and other variants. To inculcate in all its real followers and to inspire them for an ideal living in peaceful co-existence and philanthropic understanding are thus the aims of religions of the world. Activities isolated from these basic aims of religions can not be considered as religious at least from the standpoint of cultural purity and may be affirmed as irreligious defilement of the real human virtue. Defilement of the human virtue results from the selfish gratification of his purposeful ends. Unity in diversities, realisation of one and the only one Noumenon in the entire phenomenal world, perception of Absolute, Ultimate and Supreme truth in various interpretations of the Omnipresent One in all and all in that one are thus the aims of all religions.

Jagannāth representing a grand synthesis of all the noumenal variants of different religions witnesses in Him the embodiment of unity in diversities. The primary concept of Jagannāth as a deity probably originated in the lap of Non-Āryan culture, when the Śavaras being the early settlers on the lands of Orissa began the magalithic worship of their departed ancestors as early as the first century of the Christian era. Legend suggesting the primary veneration of Lord Jagannāth by Śavaras and His Śavara-origin is described by the early poets of ancient oriya literature and is invariably believed by the people of Orissa as a fact. This legend while indicating the institutionalisation of this cult describes the matrimony of the Śavara bride Lalitā the daughter of Viśvābasu and the Brāhmin bridgroom Vidyāpati to whom the King Indradyumna had sent to trace out the image of Nīlamādhava, the original Śavara icon of Lord Jagannāth. The Daitāpatis—a group of servants of the temple of Lord Jagannāth at Puri observes even in this present age the funeral rites of the forsaken old images of Jagannāth as a son or successor performs that of his father, mother or predecessor. Daitāpatis also called Daitās are believed as the descendents of Vidyāpati and Lalitā and are probably named so from the term Duhitāpati. Duhitā meaning daughter points out Lalitā and Pati meanig husband points out Vidyāpati and the successors who traced out their origin from their matrimonial union are called Duhitāpat is or Dayitāpatis. Originated in the lap of the Non-Āryan culture of the Śavaras, the image of Lord Nīlamādhava was probably named as Jaganta or Jagnāilā also. The Śavaras in Orissa call their God as Kituṇg and attribute Him with ten forms-Jaganta or Jagnāilā, Toḍ, Tuman, Bhim, Raṇgraṇg Garsīd, Raman, Jajepal, Matta and Titi. Scholars have tried to trace out the origin of Lord Jagannāth from the age of Ṛig Veda by an arbitrary interpretation of the Ṛig Vedic verse 10/155/3.

"Āde Yaddāru plavate Sindhupāre apouruṣam, Tena rabhasva durhaṇe lena gachchha parastaraṁ."

As this verse doeṣ not indicate a little of Lord Jagannāth in distinctive certainty and as Orissa in any of its ancient nomenclatures does not figure in the known literature of early Ṛig vedic age, it seems unreasonable to congrue with the view of these scholars. Bhāgavatism seems to have been popular in Kaliṇga when the Māṭhara kings of Orissa held the reins of Government in fourth century A. D. The Māṭharas, were the devotees of their 'Bappabhaṭṭārakas' or departed ancestors and Ananta Śaktivarman a prominent king of this dynasty was a worshipper of both Nārayanasvāmī and his departed ancestor as it is known from his Andhavaram plates. Vaiṣṇavite influence probably crept into the cult of the Śavara God Jaganta or Jagnāilā or Nīlamādhava during this period. Mahābhārata, reasonably believed to have been composed in its different sections in between Fourth century B. C. and Fourth century A. D. (M. Winternitz—A History of Indian Literature Vol—I Munshiram Manoharlal New Delhi 1972 pp. 474-475) describes Mādhava a Vaiṣṇavite God as a deity of Mauna (Silence) dhyāna (contemplation) and Yoga (meditation) the elements of esoteric nature. Esoteric practices followed invariably by the Śavaras are called popularly as Savarīvidyā. Corroborative testimenies from heterogenous sources (R. P. Mishra—Sahajayāna—A study of Tāntric Buddhism, Punthi Pustak, Calcutta 1991 pp. 270-278) reveal that the legshapped Śavara deity Jaganta or Jagnāilā or Nīlamādhava achieved probably an institutional enshrinement when the Non-Āryan Bhaumakaras obtained this deity from the Śavaras, got it carved into three prominent images, retained in these images both the iconic feature and aniconic symbolism as a sign of the amalgam of both Āryan and Non-Āryan cultures and enshrined these images in an ordinary temple in Puri. By the time of the composition of Anargharāghavaṁ by paundit Murārī Mishra in 8th-9th century A. D. Jagannāth associated with Mahālakṣhmī of Māṇavasā Tradition and named as puruṣhottama was already worshipped on the shore of the salty sea of Puri. Mahālakṣhmī was called Kamalā also during this period. On the ruins of the Bhauma temple of Lord Jagannāth, the Somavaṁśī king Yayāti-I also built an ordinary temple to continue the institutionalisation of this cult. After the death of Yayāti-I, royal patronage to this cult was probably not so profound till the rule of Anantavarmā choḍagaṅgadeva as the Dasgoba copper plate inscription of this king suggests. The cult of Jagannāth attained the acme of popularity in the midst of unprecedented ceremonial institutionalisation when in Eleventh century A. D. choḍagaṅgadeva built the present Jagannāth temple. By this time Jagannāth as puruṣottama had already been considered as the Transcendent parambrahman as the Dasgoba copper plate inscriptions describes. What this inscription describes with regard to His transcendent Brahman nature is given below.

"Pādou yasyadharāntarīkṣha makhilaṁ
Nābhiṣu Sarvādiśah
Śrotraṁ netrayugaṁ ravīndu yugalaṁ
Murddhnāpicha dyaurasau

Prāsādam puruṣottamasya Nṛipate
Konāmaṁ Karttuṁ Kṣhamah
Tasyeitādya nṛipeirupekṣhitamayaṁ,
Chakretha Gangeśvarah"

The cult of Lord Jagannāth developed unique sense of assimilative toleration from the beginning of its evolution. This assimilative toleration elevated the popularity of this cult among the Non-Āryan, Āryans, Śaivas, Śāktas, Vaiṣṇavas, Sauras, Gāṇapatyas, Jainas, Buddhists, Tāntric Buddhists, Muslims, Christians. and the followers of many other religions. Śavaras worshipped Him as Jagantā or Jaganāilā or Nīlamādhava, Gandas of Orissa worshipped Him as Jaṇgā, Bandos and Gadba prayed Him as Viṣṇu, Sauras beheld the manifestation of Sun in His eyes and the Gāṇapatyas found in Him the embodiment of Gaṇeśa. He appeared as Trīratnas to the Jainas, Trīśaraṇas to the followers of Early Buddhism and Mahāyāna, the Brāhmanical Tāntrists found in Him Avyakta, Vyakta and Prakṛiti and also the guides of Divya, Vīra and Paśu modes of Tāntric realisations. The Tāntric Buddhists perceived in His holy triad the Kāya-Vajra Vak-vajra and Chitta-vajra the combination of which according to Śrī Guhyasamāja Tantra constitutes the nature of Vajrasattva, the Tāntric Buddhist noumenon and that of Hindu Trinity. Indrabhuti invokes Lord Jagannāth as adorable by all Jinas, as the primal source of all Buddhas and their perfect enlightenments and as omnipresent as the sky. Sāralā Dās delineates Jagannāth of Nīlāchala or Puri or Puruṣettamakṣhetra as the incarnation of Buddha and also as Hindu Trinity. Āchārya Śhaṇkara while visiting Puri in Ninth century A.D established here the Bhogavarddhan Maṭha because of the popularity of Lord Jagannāth, Rāy Rāmānanda the preacher of Vaiṣṇavism, Kavīra the preacher of Bhakti movement Nānak the founder of Śikhism, Chaitanya the founder of Gauḍīya Vaiṣṇavism, Rāmānuja the preacher of Vaiṣṇavism and Sādhu Sundar Dās the preacher of Christianity in Orissa traced in Jagannāth the manifestation of the supremest truth of their faiths. Sālbeg the son of Muslim father Lālbeg and the Brahmin mother resided in Puri and prayed Lord Jagannāth by composing devotional songs of alluring emotional appeal. Even to-day in the neeks and corners people repeat with devotion the Bhajans or the devotional songs of this Yavana poet. Even at present in Puri the cars of Jagannāth halt for a moment near the tomb of Sālbeg. Because of the unique assimilative toleration and encouragement of the human values by this cult Jagannāth figures in different views of human considerations. He appears as a beggar in Oriya Māṇavasā Lakṣhmī purāṇa because of his fault and inspite of his divine supremacy. While seeking a mythical association of the Dāru or Log of Jagannāth, the Orissan legend considers this Dāru as the unburnt portion of the forsaken body of Lord Śrīkṛiṣhṇa after his demise. This Dāru or unburnt portion as the legend of Orissa suggests is described as a defiled part of the body of this Lord with sin. What Saralā Dās writes in Mahābhārat about this part is given below.

> "Goṣṭhe thilāvele Vakā Ṣaṇḍhā chanti māri
> Valatkāre harithile Gopīgaṇa dhari
> Jiva thivājae Tānku pāpa na lāgilā
> Maraṇa pare e piṇḍe kalaṇka rahilā"

Kavisurya Baladeva Ratha described Jagannāth as a malevolent snake but while criticising so he traced in the cult of Jagannāth a greatness of cosmic and philanthropic value. Observing the violation of assimilative tolerance among the temple dignitaries of Puri and the Mihimāites in a tussle although Bhima Bhoi in chapter 95 of his Stuti Chintāmaṇi rebukes puruṣottama the Kṣhetra as well as the God Jagannāth he does not hesitate to pray this god with devotion in chapter-VIII of his work. Lord Jagannāth as his devoted followers believe not only represent a magnanimous concept of religion but also a growing greatness of Orissan polity, Orissa during the age of Imperial Gaṇgas was called puruṣottama Sāmrājya or empire of puruṣottama. The Imperial Gaṇga king Anaṇgabhimadeva-III described himself in his charter as puruṣottama-putra and Rāuta of Lord Jagannāth. Rāuta means a deputy of the king. All these elements in the cult of Jagannāth suggest that it is an excellent human culture beyond the narrowness of sectarian consideration and has many things to be learned by the humanity for the global and human unity and what to speak of National Integrity ? Religions have to teach and not to impose. We have to learn, follow and not to violate what is considered as unimpeachable good. If this is done in better understanding the teachings of the cult of Jagannāth will undoubtedly be a milestone towards National and human unity and understanding. Learned discourse of Dr. Mohanty is really instructive and commendable in this regard.

From seventh century A. D. onwards Tāntric Buddhism flourished in Oḍḍiyāna or Uḍḍiyāna with an esoteric system of Sādhanā promulgated by a group of Siddhas or Āchāryas. These Tāntric teachers gave importance to Kriyās (rite and rituals) charyās (mystical practices) Yoga (meditation) and Anuttara yoga (the transcendental meditation) and established the identity of Saṁsāra (the living in the phenomenal world) with the highest Truth of their faiths to which they called Vajra, Sahaja or Kālachakra in their doctrines. Their new systems knows as Vajrayāna, Sahajayāna, and Kālachakrayāna taught different kinds of yogic theories and practices for the realisation of Buddha-hood. Buddha-hood as these Tāntric schools suggests is a state of perfect enlightenment which enables the adherent to realise the Śunyatā nature or indefinableness of every thing. Śunyatā does not denote here a Nothingness, a nihilism, an empty void or a negative abyss,

Every thing is called śunya because of its Śunyatā nature which is indefinable and indepictable. Śunyatā is relative as well as real. In Tāntric Buddhism every thing is Sunya appearances are svabhāva Śunya or devoid of ultimate reality and ultimate reality is prapanchaśunya or devoid of plurality. Śunya is thus Saṁsāra as well as Nirvāṇa. The Tāntric Buddhists accept Bodhi or Pure consciousness as Ultimate Reality. Tāntric Buddhism thus combines in its doctrine the Śunyatā doctrines of the Mādhyamika and the doctrine of Alaya Vijnāna or Abhutparikalpa in its doctrinal elucidation. As it suggests, a perfect knowledge of Śunyatā by theoretical cognition and yogic perception generates a state of Mahāsukha or supreme Bliss which is concomitant with Buddhahood. Buddhahood enables the adherent to realise the absolute and Non-dual Truth that everything-in-universe and Universe-in-everything are one and the same and are the manifestation of Śunyatā or Vajra or Sahaja or Kālachakra which is beyond origination, destruction and all illusive mentation of discriminative nature. Tāntric Buddhism believes every phenomena as a miniature universe or a microcosmic representation of the illimitable cosmos and the Universe as the macrocosm of all these microcosms. This Buddhism considers all men as relative embodiments of primal Buddha Vajrasattva and all women as the relative manifestation of Prajnā the inseparable Śakti of this primal Buddha Vajrasattva. In this Buddhism adherents are advised to eliminate from their minds all thoughts of illusive discriminations and thus to develop a sense of perfect equality towards all. Indrabhuti while describing Jagannāth as adorable by all Jinas probably indicates the removal of Sectarian narrowness from religion. Jina here does not mean Jain but all who have subdued their evil proclivities. Indrabhuti was the Vajrayānist king of Saṁbalaka, the modern Sambalpur in Orissa. Lakṣhmīṇkarā the sister of the king Indrabhuti advised all not to have women irrespective of caste, creed and colour as the relative manifestations of Prajnā. Better elements of human equality and unity are thus conspicuously traceable in the tenets of Tāntric Buddhism. This Buddhism may ably serve the cause of better human understanding, equality of all men and their unity if its ethics are translated into action. Oḍḍiyāna reasonably identified with Orissa was the cradle land of Tāntric Buddhism. From Oḍḍiyāna this Buddhism travelled to different parts of India and even abroad.

Bhakti as a concept of Indian religion goes back to a remote antiquity although the Bhakti movement as a religious movement of reformative value took its birth in the medieval age of Indian History. Bhakti derived from the Sanskrit root—Bhaj+Ktin—generally from the etymological sense signifies first to serve and revere and then to love and profess devotion. Bhakti in the sense of love and devotion occurs in a verse of Śvetāśvatara upaniṣad. In Bhagvad Gitā in chapter-XII Bhakti while denoting worship, love and devotion of God also signifies selfless and absolute surrender to God through love, devotion, self-control and sacrifice. The Nārāyaṇīya section of Mahābhārata which reasonably considered as a later work than Bhagvad Gitā by Dr. M. Winternitz (A History of Indian Literature New Delhi 1972 Vol-I P. 439) teaches that perfection can only be attained by Bhakti and the grace of God. In Bhāgavatism Navadhā Bhaktis or Nine types of Bhaktis are described. These nine types of Bhaktis are described as :

> "Śravaṇaṁ Kirttanaṁ Viṣṇor Smaraṇam
> Pādasevanaṁ. —Archanaṁ Vandanaṁ
> dāsyaṁ Sakhyaṁ Ātmanivedanaṁ."

Śravaṇa as the first type of Bhakti denotes the devotional hearing of the tales of the life, teachings and achievements of God. Kirtanaṁ means the devotional discourse on His life, teachings and achievements. Smaranaṁ signifies the devotional mentation or contemplation of the God with a strong concentration. Pādasevaṇam means service at the feet of the God.

Archanam means devotional veneration. Vandanam means devotional prayers. Dāsyam is explained as most obedient and faithful service. Sakhyaṁ signifies devotional friendship. Atmanivedanam connotes selfless and absolute surrender to God with love and devotion. The Bhāgabatas theorise that King Parīkṣhita achieved perfection in Bhakti by hearing God's life, teaching and achievements, Vaiyāsaki or Śukadeva attained it by narrating those of the God, Prahlāda possessed it by His devotional contemplation, Lakṣhmī owned by her service at His feet, Pṛithu realised it by devotional worship, Akrura availed it by devotional prayer, Hanumān the devotee of Lord Rāma obtained it by his faithfull and obedient service, Arjuna became capable of achieving it by devotional friendship and Valīrājā or the king Valī owned it by self-less and devotional surrender.

Indian Bhakti movement of the mediaeval age while basing its structural points on various elements like the theory of Vedāntas, yogas, love, devotion and mysticism preached the fundamental equality of all religions and the unity of Godhead. It professed that the dignity of man depends on the nature of action and on his heredity. It rejected the caste-discrimination and untouchability as a mere folly. It protested against excessive ritualism and formalities of religion and asserted that these things are really unnecessary for realising the Supreme Truth. It emphasised on moral living, simplicity of behaviour, equal vision towards all, service of the creature, virtuous way of thinking and working and devotional love towards God as the means of unfailing salvation and the realisation of the supreme truth. It finds no difference between Krishṇa and Karīm, Rāma and Rahīm, Ā-llāh and Ātman, Muslim and Hindus, Brahmin and Śudra and says that in the eyes of God everybody is equal and that any discrimination is a sin against His law of creation. Rāya Rāmānanda, Rāmānuja, Mādhava or Ānandatīrtha, Nimbārka, Kavīr, Ballabhāchārya, Chaitanya,

Nānaka, Nāmdev, Tukārām and many others were the protagonists, preachers and philosophers of this Bhakti movement. The Bhakti movement thus had an integrative and reformative value for the better living and peaceful co-existence of men besides its religious message for equality of all religions.

Many of the saints of Bhakti movement visited Orissa in course of their travel to Puri or Puruṣottama Kṣhetra for preaching and popularising their doctrines. Orissa inspired by an assimilative trend of religious amalgam since the days of Indrabhuti and Bhaumakara kings had reposed the laudable consecration of this trend in the cult of Lord Jagannāth. The Bhakti Saints observing a lofty function of their ideals in this cult perceived the identity of their supreme truth in Lord Jagannāth and their doctrines exerted profound influence on the folklore in the nooks and the corner of O-rissa in their accultured or remodelled form. In many respects the analysis of Dr. Dolagobinda Bishi seems appreciable.

Mattamayūra Śaivism originated in the lap of Śaivasiddhānta school in Delhi-Kurukṣhetra region travelled to Orissa in course of its spread to different parts of India. Āmarddakatīrthanātha Rudraśambhu, Mattamayūranātha purandara, Sadāśiva, vyomaśiva-I, Pataṇgaśiva or Pataṇgaśambhu, Gaganaśiva II and other Mattamayūra Śaiva ascetics really popularised this Śaivism in different parts of Orissa. The Nāga King Śatrubhanja the Śailodbhavas, the Somavaṁśīs, the Eastern Gaṇgas and the kings of many other ruling dynasties of Orissa accorded royal patronage to this Śaivism.

Mattamayūra Śaivism while professing the māntric and Yogic worship of Paramaśiva believes in the spiritual elevation of all its adherents from the lowest grade of Apakvakaluṣa Sakala Jiva to the highest stage of Muktātmaśiva by Yogic perfection. This śaivism nourishes credence, in the potentiality of every individual for realising Śiva-hood or Śivatva although it asserts that a Muktātmaśiva or free-soul Śiva seeks the mercy of Paramaśiva the supremest Reality of this Śaivism even after this realisation. As this Śaivism asserts, Caste, colour, material status and other illusive discrimination do not figure as a bar in achieving this Śivatva if the adherent follows the prescribed practice of this Śaivism properly. In extending this equal treatment towards all and in considering the body of every individual as a temple, the Jiva or the vitality of everybody as Sadāsiva or Eternal Śiva and service to others as the best of all virtues this Śaivism really professes an unimpeachable doctrine of Humanism the best of all 'isms' in the world. What this Śaivism describes in the voice of paramaśiva is quoted below.

"yo mām drakṣhati sarveṣu
Sarvān sevete Niṣpruha
Karoti parakalyāṇam
Tyaktvā sarva Vikalpakaṁ
Sabhabet Siddhamantrī cha
Bhedābheda Vivarjitah
Muktātmabhāva Samyogāt
Prapnoti paramaṁ padaṁ
Deham devālayaṁ proktaṁ
Jivah deva Sadāśivah
Tasmāt paropakāraṁ hi
Sarvadharma Śreyaṣkaraṁ"

It is doubtless that the unimpeachable practice of this Philanthropical doctrine can establish with all certainties the perfect peace, tranquility and happy living of all in this world.

The cult of the Goddess Lakṣhmī of the Māṇavasā Tradition in Orissa seems as a cult of remote antiquity although it finds a popular recognition in Oriyā Lakṣhmī purāṇa composed by poet Balarām Dās in Sixteenth century A. D. From the worship of Paddy in this cult the nomenclature of this cult as the Dhāŋamāṇika Lakṣhmī worship and the observation of this cult in the month of harvest, this cult rightly appears to have originated from the aggrarian culture of Orissa since a remote antiquity. The Oriya Lakṣhmī purāṇa while describing the reverential process of this cult cites reference to the faithful service of Vetāla and miraculous power of Lakṣhmī in causing hardship for Lord Jagannāth and Balarām. That Orissa was a citadel of Śāktaism and Tāntricism associated with the cult of Vetāls is undoubtedly proved by the Vaitāla temple of Bhubaneśvar which is generally accepted as an antiquity of eighth century A. D. The presiding deity of this temple is the terrific Chāmuṇḍā whose tāntric cult was associated with that of Vetālas who are generally believed as the media of Kāpālika for attaining Siddhi. In Devī Māhātmya of Mārkandeya purana śakti figures as Chāmuṇḍā and Mahā Lakṣhmī is described as primal Śakti in prādhānika rahasyaṁ of Śrī Durgāsaptaśati another variant of the tāntric application of this Devī Māhātmya. In Devī Māhātmya the Śakti of Viṣṇu is called Vaiṣṇavī with her vehicle as Garuḍa. In vaitāla temple of Bhubanesvar Vaiṣṇavī or Nārāyaṇī Mātṛikā while showing her the āyudha or weapon as those of Viṣṇu displays in her pedestal a human figure with the left-hand upraised instead of Garuḍa. This reasonably suggests that the cult of Vaiṣṇavī or Lakshmī in Orissa was accompanied by a left-handed practice of Tāntric worship. As Śakti saŋgama Tantra describes, the land stretching from the Kṣhetra of Jagannāth to the bank of river Kṛiṣhnā is called Kaliŋga and is a land of left-handed practice. In clear contrast to the Vegetarian taste of Kriṣhṇa and Balarām elseshere in India the Oriyā Lakṣhmī Purāṇa describes Jagannāth and Balarām as lover of Mṛigayā or hunting in dense forest. The Devī Māhātmya describes yoganidra as Śakti of Viṣṇu. Brahmā while desiring the rise of Viṣṇu from deep slumber prays yoganidrā in Devī Māhātmya as Śrī or Lakṣhmī and describes Viṣṇu as Jagatsvāmī which is synonymous with Jagannāth. In Oriyā Lakṣhmī purāṇa Lakṣhmī sends Nidravati for causing slumber in the eyes of Jagannāth and Balarām. In Suvarna prabhāsa sūtraṁ a Mahāyānic text the worship of Śrīmahādevī as a goddess of good harvest of Paddy, wealth and prosperity is described in chapter-IX called Śrīmahādevīparivartta. In this chapter it is clearly suggested that the veneration of Śrī Mahādevī must be performed in the hands of the worshipper and not by engaging priests, Śrī Mahādevī in this chapter is named as Śrīya Mahādevī also. In chapter-XI of this Mahāyānic text, reference is cited to Śrī or Lakṣhmī many times while it describes the worship of Earth as a goddess. Chapter-XI is named as Dṛḍhāpṛithivīparivartta. Suvarnaprabhāsa Sutraṁ with all its interpolations is considered as a work of Eighth century A. D. All these facts from different sources reveal that the cult of Lakṣhmī in a Tāntric apperance prevailed in Orissa as early as eighth century A. D. It is probable that the cult of Māṇavasā Lakṣhmī appeared in a dominant Vaiṣṇavite colour in later time and Balarām Dās while delineating its vaiṣṇavite nature in consociation with the cult of Jagannāth did not ignore its original Tāntric nature.

The Māṇavasā Tradition of Lakṣhmī worship of Orissa teaches for the maintenance of the purity and cleanness of the house, for the morality and discipline in family life and for a better understanding between the members of the house. It also professes a strong reaction against the discrimination of caste in the worship of the Gods and Goddesses. It asserts the right of woman in equal footing with that of man in respectful apperance in public life. It affirms that worshippers irrespective of their birth, caste, wealth and social status can achieve the grave of Gods or Goddesses. In professing such lofty ideals of family and society buildings, the cult of Orissan Māṇavasā Lakṣhmī embodies an integrative value of human living and better social life. Dr. Upendranath Mohanty really brings out a praiseworthy analysis of this cult in terms of these human values.

The Kandhas as a representative community of Indian Tribal society had developed a miraculous way of beliefs and practices in congruence with that of the Indian Tribal Society from remote antiquity. Such beliefs and practices whatever may be their philosophical meaning formed the primary concept of Tantra. Indian Tantras while professing paśu, vīra and Divya modes of Sādhanā begins from the gross material worship and enables the worshipper to attain highest spiritual truth in divya way of Sādhanā. Dr. Dolagobinda Bishi has really collected some of the oblivious informations on the obscure Kandha practices of magical rites which generally become helpful in studying the tāntric evolution.

As there is a puranic saying in India "religion teaches man is hoped to follow and the teaching of religion bears fruits when it is really implemented into proper practice" True it is, knife used in surgery saves life while its misuse by a murderer destroys life. Religion can assure peaceful co-existence, better human understanding and social solidarity only when its ethics will be properly applied with a philanthropic aspiration.

It is desirable that we have yet to learn and practise many things from religions the intellectual products of our ancient seers, sages, prophets and teachers.

Independence Day
Titilagarh
15th August 1993

Dr. Ramprasad Mishra
Editor

NATIONAL INTEGRATION IN INDIA AND THE CULT OF LORD JAGANNATH

1

NATIONAL INTEGRATION IN INDIA AND THE CULT OF LORD JAGANNATH

Dr. U. N. Mohanty

Principal, D. A. V. College Titilagarh

For few past years, it has been almost a routine on our parts to skip on some of the glaring headlines in our daily news papers pertaining to fresh disturbances in the state of Punjab, killing of innocent people by the socalled terrorists, regionalism raising its ugly head in Maharastra, Assam, Kashmir and in many other States in much varied and virulent forms.

India is a multi-religious country. The Hindus, the Muslims, the Buddhists and the Jains all enjoy their modes of religious life independently. There are a number of branches also existing in Hindu religion. All her religious are inextricably fused with its social and cultural patterns. They suggest moral codes and man's social behaviour. One of the distinct sects among Hindus is Vaisnavism, it has its own trends and beliefs.

Vaiṣṇavism believes in one God as that is Viṣṇu who is known variously as Nāṛāyaṇa, Kṛiṣhṇa, vāsudeva-Kṛiṣhṇa and Gopāl-Kṛiṣhṇa etc. The origin of Vaiṣṇavism or worship of Viṣhṇu has been traced back even to the Vedic age and this Visnu, the supreme God in course of time took different Avatāras or incarnations. As regards the evolution of religious ideas, we find from available sources that the earlier form of Vaiṣṇavism was more or less ethical, but afterwards this ethical nature has slightly changed. The cult of devotion or Bhakti which might have its origin in earlier period, gradually took on a new orientation when amatory qualities were emphasized in the Gitagovinda of Jayadeva by the end of the 12th century A. D. This orientation in Bhakti-cult which began by the end of the 12th century A. D. gradually spread over Indian sub-continent by different preachers.[1] The impact and influence of this Bhakti cult on the Indian society was much more greater than any other religious ideas.

One of the results of Bhakti or rather one of its characteristics has been described as the oneness of all with self (Sarvātmabhāva).[2] Through the deep notion of love one sees every soul as one's beloved, God being all, it is natural that through intense attachment to Him one should perceive Him in all things, for these are all manifestations of God. If this essence of Bhakti is spread among the Indian citizens, the problem of National Integration may be solved to a greater extent.

Orissa has exhibited the panorama of different religious scences and the flow of religious trends that flows since remote time. In the pre-christian period Jainism was the most important non-indigenous religion in Orissa. Although it lost royal support in the Ist century A. D. after the downfall of the Mahameghabāhana dynasty, its roots in the population were deep and in Kalinga it retained its dominant position up to the end of the 7th century A. D. Buddhism, after an unsuccessful attempt in the time of Ashoka started to gain group in Orissa from Ist century A. D. onwards. It was flourising about 641 A. D. when Hiuen Tsang visited the country. In its Vajrayana form it reached the height of prosperity under the Bhaumakara rulers in the 8th-10th centuries. Thereafter, Buddhism gradually declined, but not as quickly as in other parts of India. Śaivism was the dominating religion in Central Orissa from the 6th century onwards and reached the peak of its glory during the Somavaṁśī rule in the 10th and 11th centuries.

Śāktism was closely related to Śaivism although its traces may reach back to an even more distinct past. The period when the Śāktas gained their greatest influence and were most generously supported by the rulers of Orissa extended from the 8th to the 11th centuries.[3]

Though it is very difficult to ascertain the exact date of the origin of Vaiṣṇavism or Viṣṇu worship in Orissa, yet it can be said with utmost sincerity that it had its origin during the Māṭhara dynasty reigned from 350 A. D. to 440 A. D. The Vaisnavism during the period under review was the principal religion of the people of the kingdom as it has been proved from archaeological evidences. The King Prabhanjana-varman in his Nengondi copper plate grant declared himself as the devotee of Nārāyaṇa.[4] Gradually the particular religious tradition became popular among the people spreading spontaneously from one corner to another and surpassing the other religious beliefs.

We know that from eleventh century A. D. Puri became the preaching ground of Vaiṣṇavism, Religious life in Orissa has been dominated by the cult of Puruṣottama Jagannāṭh ever since the famous and majestice present temple of Lord Jagannāth in Puri was built by Choḍagaṇga Dev in the 12th century A. D. According to tradition this temple replaced an earlier one which had run in to decay.

It is said that the history of the religion of the people of Orissa, is so to say, the history of Lord Jagannāth, due to the existence of Lord Puruṣottam-Jagannāth, the Puruṣottam Kṣhetra i. e., Puri attained the highest pitch of its glory and for its sanctity it is considered as the Vaikuntha Dham of Bhagaban Visnu Jagannāth in various Puranas.[5] This Kṣhetra is not only a sacred place for the Vaiṣṇavas, but is equally for Śaivas, Śāktas, Gāṇapatyas, Jainas and even for the Buddhists. The shrine of Lord Jagannāth has not only become a centre of attraction for the pilgrims, but the mysterious nature of the cult itself has inspired the scholars to take up serious research in different aspects of this religious institution.

The cult of lord Jagannāth has the potentiality of integrating all religions, castes, creeds, cults and colours, because this cult is unique and incomparable in its assimilative toleration and universal appeal. For the Jainas Jagannāth is the 'Jīna' for Buddhists he is 'Buddha' for Śaivites he is the 'Bhairava', and for Vaiṣṇavas he is 'Viṣṇu' Saint Tulasī Dās found Ram in Him, Mahātmā Śrī Chaitanya found 'Kṛiṣhṇa' in Him. He is the God of Gāṇapatya sect, Guru N-ānak had his monastery near Śrīmandira. Kavīr had established his 'Chhatā' there. There are a few instances of how the cult of Lord Jagannāth has brought about the integration of religions of the past which survived till date. In fact no religion, no cult, no creed flourished in India without having its monastery at Jagannāth Dhām. It appears as if Jagannāth Dhām Ie., Puri is the religious capital of India and these religious monasteries found in Śhrī Kṣhetra are like the embassies of other religions, sects cults at this religious capital.

The evolution of the cult of Lord Jagannāth is sorrounded by impenetrable mysteries. The Scholars have failed to answer many questions relating to Lord Jagannāth. There is a culture which is represented by Lord Jagannāth, whether this culture developed first and then emerged Lord Jagannāth as the physical embodiment of this culture, is a very important question which is unanswered yet.

Lord Jagannāth is the beautiful combination of various faiths prevailing in the country from time to time. The Jagannāth cult incorporates in it all the ideas, ideologies doctrines, theology and tradition of different sects, philosophers and preachers. He has been considered by some as an aboriginal Tribal God, while He had appeared to some as a Buddhist incarnation, a Tantric Saivite God, as the Param Brahma, the very embodiment of the Lord on the earth in form of a Dāru.

Jagannāth does not belong to any particular religion, sect or group, Jagannāth Dharma is the outcome of various religious trends from the pre-Vedic period to the modern age and assimilates in it different rituals theology, traditions and doctrines. He is the unique synthesis of Buddhist, Jaina, Śaivite, Tāntric and Vaiṣṇavite elements while he has been associated with pre-historic and Tribal Gods.

The wooden body of Lord Jagannāth reminds us of the oustom of tree-worship of the ancient Drāviḍians in Indus-valley civilisation. The Śabaras of Orissa used to worship their God 'Jaganta' and perhaps the word Jagannāth has been derived from the word 'Jaganta' the name of a tree. The iconography of Jagannāth triad is very closely associated with the aniconic worship of Śabara-origin of the remote past. Regarding the Śabara-worship of Lord Jagannāth many foreign and native historians have expressed similar views which testify to the aboriginal element of Lord Jagannāth. The special class of Sevāyatas (servants) known as 'Daitās' of Jagannāth is believed to be descendants of early Śabaras.[9] Scholars have identified Jagannāth with Buddha and the later had occupied the ninth position in tenincarnations of Lord Viṣṇu. The legendary tradition narrates that the tooth relic of Lord Buddha has been placed inside the wooden image of Jagannath, which is believed to be the that mysterious 'Nābhi-Kamala' or 'Brahma', the supreme self. The eminent Buddhist scholar Indrabhuti in the beginning of his book 'Jñānasiddhi' invoked Lord Jagannāth as 'Praṇipatya Jagannātham Sarbajīna barārchittaṁ, Sarbabuddhamayaṁ Siddhi byāpinaṁ gaganopamaṁ.' The first Oriya epic poet Sarala Das in his Mahābhārat on many occasions has described Jagannath as 'Buddha'.

So also historians attribute Jain element to the evolution of Jagannāth-cult and assert the claim on Jagannath as the deity of the Jains. The word Jagannath according to them is derived from the Jaina-deity 'Jināsana' or 'Jananāth' similarly the city of Pithuṇḍa, a center of Jaina-worship in Kalinga, is believed to be that of Puri. The Car-festival of lord Jagannāth on the 2nd day of bright moon in the month of Ashadha and His bathing-festival (Snānayātrā) have amazing resemblance with those of the Jains. Prevalence of Kaivalya and Kalpabriksha is also due to Jaininfluence.

The Saiva-componens in the rituals and theological evolution of Jagannāth-cult are corelated with the doctrines of Tāntrism and Śākta-Dharma. The scholars had found iconographical affinity between the peculiar appearance of Jagannath and Siva, who is worshipped as Bhairaba, in His fierce-aspect (Ugrarupa). Particularly the sculptural representations of Ekapada Bhairava (Someswar temple, Mukhalingam, 9th century show a striking similarity with the Jagannath image, especially with the earliest extant representation of Jagannath from Konarka.[7] Similarly the Tantric-literary texts identify Jagannath with Mahabhairava.[8] The representation of Sri Balabhadra in the Jagannath-triad as Sankarsana or Sesanaga in His Saivite-manifestation, is another testimony to the Saivite element of Jagannath cult. Likewise the third deity Subhadra representin the Saktaelement, is still worshipped with Bhubaneswari-mantra even when the Vaisnava-movement became prominent. Jagannath Balabhadra, Subhadra have been defined as Visnu, Siva and Durga respectively.[9]

The Tantric element in Jagannath-cult has occupied a prominent place and Srikshetra (Puri) has been narrated as a seat of Tantric worship (Tantrapitha) in Tantras and Puranas. In the Tantric texts Jagannath is identified with Mahabhairava and Goddess Vimala is His Sakti. The Prasad of Lord Jagannath becomes Mahaprasad only after it is reoffered to Goddess Vimala. Similarly different Tantric features of Yantras have been engraved on the Ratnavedi where Jagannathtriad are consecrated. Even now the Sakta-modes of rituals and theology are still prevailing.

The vaisnative element has been the most important feature in the Jagannath—cult. Since the reign of Ananta-Varma Chodagangadev i. e., 12th century A. D. Jagannath has been Vaisnavised. Odissi—Vaisnavism has reached a point of culmination passing through a process of evolution of different forms, rituals abd vekuefs cibterubg ariybd Kird Jagannath. In the list of the differen forms of Lord Visnu, Krishna-Vesudev is the most popular one and in Post-Chaitanya period. Krisna became the most prominent deity. This Krishna-Vasudeva form of Visnu has been identified with Lord Jagannath,

Another important Vaisnavite typology of Hinduism is the form of Madhava the later form of Krisna-Vasudeva. The introduction of Madhava-worship in Orissa is very old and the iconographical evidences at Prachi-Valley in Puri district and Balangir district of western Orissa testify to that effect. According to mythological and legendary traditions, Jagannath was worshipped as Nilamadhava at Nilachala by the Sabara King Viswavasu the descendant of Jara, who assassinated Krisna at Dwaraka. Indradyumna the Vaisna king of Malva in the quest of Nilamadhava deputed his Brahmin Minister Vidyapati who located Hi with the help of Lalita, daughter of Visvavasu. But the image of Nilamadhava vanished before the king had got His glimpse and reappeared in the form of Daru in Orissa.

The Ganga Kings, specially Ananta Varman Chodagangadeva had emphasised the Vaisnavic element of Jagannath and with the construction of the existing temple, later's Vaisnavic feature became prominent. The Panchasakha-age ie., 16th century A. D. again gave impetus to the Vaisnava-movement, which was ultimately absorbed in Jagannath cult. Sri Chaitanya he founder of neo-Vaisnavism in Bengal found the dual image of Radha-Krishna in the image of Lore Jagannath. Thus the Jagannath cult has been a beautful combination of Various faiths prevailing in Orissa and abroad from time to time consisting of the tribal, Buddhist Jaina, Saivite and Tantric elements an conclusively took the Vaisnavic form to the fullest extent. The Jagannath-cult has absorbed different views, doctrines of different theologians and preachers in it and at the same time preached the idea of universalism, the thought of catholicism and brotherhood in the world. This is now the cult of Lord Jagannath is the meeting ground of different religions, sects, etc.

Similarly in the caste-based Indian society, the cult of Lord Jagannath exceptionally had the capability of uniting all the castes creeds in a systematic way. Hatred, discrimination' un-touchability etc. were chief characteristics of Indian caste-based social life in the past. Caste-supremacy was also the cause of large scale exploitation. For this in the beginning of this century Mahatma Gandhi propagated the idea of equality, fraternity and brother-hood. He also tried to abolish untouchability from the Indian society. But long before the cult of Lord Jagannath has propagated the same idea and ideals through different festivals and rituals. There are some popular legends in which it has been depicted that in the eyes of God all human beings are equal. It tells that God loves him who loves God irrespective of his caste or social status. There are numerous stories about this and some of these stories are also included in the rituals of Jagannath worship. Two of such legends are mentioned below.

In the ancient times, untouchables have no right to worship God or read scriptures. But in the cult of Lord Jagannath it has been stated that even lowest caste has the right to worship God. There is a Purana in Oriya namely 'Laxmi Purana' on the basis of which even to-day every Oriya Hindu family worships Laxmi in the lunar month of Margasira on every Thursday irrespective of their castes. The story in short is Once Laxmi the devout wife of Jagannath went out leaving the great temple on a Thursday to have a visit to different houses in the city. She saw Sriya Chandaluni, a lady who belongs to the caste of untouchables was offering adoration to Mahalaxmi with full devotion. Mahalaxmi was very much pleased and received gladly her worship and accepted food from her hands. As this was treated as a social offence at that time. Balabhadra the eldest brother of Jagannath compelled his brother to disallow admission of Laxmi into the Srimandira Malahaxmi got furious and left Sri Mandira. As per Her request Visvakarma built a beautiful palace near the sea-beach. She sent Vetalas to Sri Mandira and took away all the wealth in the very night. Next morning when both the brothers got up, they saw that there was nothing left in the temple and no Sevakas were also present. They spent some days without food and in the temple and then decided to beg in the disguise of Brahmin. Nobody paid anything when they moved from door to door. Atlast they reached near the palace of Mahalaxmi. They were informed that it was a house of Chandala. After a futile effort of self-cooking, both the brothers took food in Mahalaxmi's house. Balabhadra realised his mistake and both the brothers begged apology. They promised that there will be no bar in worshipping Mahalaxmi in any case.

The essence of this story is that in the eyes of God nobody is high nor low. Woman has the equal right in the social life as man. Another stody is very popular in Orissa and during the car festival of Lord Jagannath, the same event is being repeated every year. It has been included as one of the rituals in the car festival. In this story how Jagannath had received a cocoanut from the hands of an untouchable has been narrated. Dasia Bauri, a low caste person once sent a cocoanut through a Brahmin to offer it to Jagannath. But that brahmin took the same and when it was offered to Lord, the cocoanut was vanished from his hand.

The Mahaparasad (cooked rice offering) can be taken by the people of all castes sitting to-gether.

The worship of Lord Jagannath was very closely connected with the royal houses of Orissa. He was the actual ruler of Orissa when as kings were just His representatives or Rauts. Thus the lords spent a royal life with Sevakas. In the pa·t the rituals of the temple were not so much as we find them now. The number was swallen up due to the gradual additions of rituals from time to time. Previously there were only 36 institutions (Chhatisa Niyogas) of temple-Servents of carry out the rituals (Seva-puja) All the castes and sub-castes in Orissa were represented within these 36 types of servants. Even though they belong to high and low castes. They are all considered to be equal in the eyes of Lord Jagannath. So that the system of hierarchy is never maintained amon the servants (Sevakas) in the temple as the duties and functions of all the servants are equally important in the performance of ritual. They are all inter-dependant and tied up together. The Raja stands at the top. But during the Car festival, the Raja performs the duty of a sweeper in front of the God in presence of Lakhs of people. Here also the cult of Lord Jagannath displays the ideals of equal social status and dignity of labour.

There were instances of non-Hindus who had great devotion to Lord Jagannath. The stody of Salabega is more historical than a legend. He was a great devotee of Lord Jagannath. He was the son of Lal Beg. The Mughal Suvedar at Cuttack under the Mughal Governmen of Delhi from 1607 to 1608.[10] Salabag's mother was a Brahmin widow to whom Lal Beg married force-fully. Sala Beg was settled in Puri and every day prayed to Lord Jagannath in singing beautiful songs composed by himself. As he was a Muslim he was no allowed to enter the temple.

So he anxiously waited to see the Lord in the Car festival. Every year he was eagerly waiting to see the Lord during the Car festival. Lord Jagannath's car was used to halt there for some time to give darsan to Salbeg. Now also his Samadhi is existing on that spot and every year cars of all three Lords are being stopped there fore some time.

Another story is recorded on Captain Albaque Beator, a French sailor, who was coming to Pondichery from Calcutta by his ship in eastern coast. A number of people belonging to France, England and India were the travellers in that Ship. The Captain came to know that a large whale is proceeding towarding towards their ship followed by a terrible storm. He was very much afraid that within a few minutes the whale and the storm will destory his ship. So he warned every body in the ship to be prepared for any eventually. Every Body in the ship was nervous. The captain saw that one person withing being nervous was praying to a portrait of some deity. When the captain asked this man, he was told that the man was praying to Lord Jagannath to protect them. Immediately the Captain told him that if Lord Jagannath will save the ship, he will stop at puri and present a huge bell which he was taking to Pondichery, in that ship. It was matter of great surprise that the captain saw through his binacular that the whale and the storm had changed their direction and the ship was saved. The captain presented the huge bell to Lord Jagannath, which was intended to be sen to Pondichery from Franne in the 18th century. Now the same bell is kept in the South Gate of the temple of Lord Jagannath.

This is how the cult of Lord Jagannath which is based on love and affection, service and sacrifice has played a vital role in uniting making belonging to various castes, creeds, colours, faiths and religions.

REFERENCES

1. The Bhakti Movement in Orissa ; A. K. Deb. Ist Edn. 1984. page-10.
2. A History of Indian Philosophy : Dr. S. N. Dasgupta Ist Edn. 1975. Page 352.
3. The cult of Jagannath and the Regional tradition of Orissa : Edt. A Eschencin Herman Kulke G. C. Tripathy Advent of Vaisnavism in Orissa by H. V. Stletencron. Page 4.
4. Inscription of Orissa : Vol. I, part-II. S. N. Rajaguru. Page-44.
5. Skanda purana-36/80.
6. Jagannath's Sabara Origin is described in Sarara Mahabharata Daru Brahma Gita of Jagannath Das and many other oriya scriptures.
7. The Saivite component in the Early Evolution of Lord Jagannath. H. V. Stletencron. (The cult of Jagannath and the Regional Tradition of Orissa) Page-120.
8. Pithanirnaya : Bharatiya Tantra Sastra, N. Mishra. Page-181.
9. Bhabishya Puran (Oriya).
10. Iqbalnama of Jahangir quoted in Journal of Indian History (Vol. XI, Page 337).

OTHER REFERENCES

Sahajayāna—A Study of Tantric Buddhism—Dr. R. P. Mishra

Jagannath in History and Religious Tradition of Orissa—
G. N. Mahapatra

Vaisnavism in Orussa : Dr. Santilata Dei

The cult of Lord Jagannath : Dr. K. C. Mishra.

TANTRIC BUDDHISM IN ORISSA

2

TANTRIC BUDDHISM IN ORISSA

Dr. Ramprasad Mishra

Notwithstanding a mass of controversial interpretations of its connotations by the authors and scholars of Tāntric theories.[1] Tantra in India is axiomatically a system of religious beliefs and practices. As a system of religious beliefs and practices Tantra is undoubtedly an esoteric cult fundamentally accompanied by its doctrine of Śakti, Mantra, Mudrā, Maṇḍalas, Makāras, Abhichāras and other mystical elements in its outersurface and a yogic practice in the inner surface in which the spiritual union on the male and female principles are propitiated for the utimate realisation of the Supreme Bliss or Supreme Reality[2] Development of Tāntra in Buddhism is generally identified as Tāntric Buddhism. Although in Tibetan Literature Buddhist Tantra is classified as Kriyā Tantra, Charyā Tantra, Yoga Tantra and Anuttara Yoga tantra[3] because of the practices of Kriyā or rites, charyā or procedure and discipline of Sādhanās, yoga or esoteric method and Annttarayoga or transcendental meditation Tāntric Buddhism is generally explained in terms of its three Schools-Vajrayāna, Sahajayāna and Kālachakrayāna. As far few discrepancies of doctrines and yogas are clearly marked in these three Tāntric Schools they are conceived as three distrinct schools and as the off shoots of Buddhist Tantrayāna[4] Dr. S. B. Dasgupta considers Vajrayāna as the composite system of Buddhist Tāntric development and Kālachakrayāna and Sahajayāna as 'Schools within it.'[5] As the earliest available Tantras of Buddhism Śrī Gūhya Samāja Tantra, Hevajra Tantra and many others while elucidating their Tāntric doctrines refer to Vajrayāna[6] and Śubhavajra or Śubhakṛiṣhṇa or Śubhākarasiṁha, Vajrabodhi and Amoghavajra while professing the doctrine of proto-Tāntric Mantrayāna or Mantranaya had in their nomenclature 'Vajra' a distinctive epithet of Buddhist Tāntric system it is possible that when in seventh century A. D. Mantrayāna was organised into a Tāntric system it assumed the nomenclature of Vajrayāna. Diametrically opposite views prevail among the scholars with regard to the time and place of the origin of Tāntric Buddhism. Prof. M. Sylvan Levi, Dr. P. C. Bagchi, Dr. B. Bhattacharya and A. B. Keith believing Asanga as the propounder of Tantra in Buddhism conceive the genesis of Tantra in Buddhism as early as the days of Asaṇga.[7] One of these scholars explaining 'Parāvṛitti of copulation' or Maithunasya parāvritte' in the work 'Mahāyānasūtrālaṇkāra' as an allusion to the mystic couples of Buddhas and Bodhisattvas believe the growth of Tantra in Buddhism during this period. P. C. Bagchi also annotating this paravritti of Mahayanasutralankara as the "enjoyment of bliss similar to that of sexual union" traces a symbolical reference to the se o-yogic practice of Buddhist Tantra in this work and suggests the development of Tantra in Buddhism as early as the time of this work and suggests the development of Tantra in Buddhism as early as the time of this Vijñānavādin author[9] Prof. Giuseppe Tucci finds a reference to one Na- ya- Siu- mo or Naya Saumo school in the work of Harivarman and Asaṇga[10] and on the basis of this finding he identifies this school with that of Somasiddhāntas which according to his view was a sect of Śaiva Kāpālikas.[11] On the basis of such identification Prof. Tucci believes the development of Tantra as early as fourth century A. D.[12] Dr. B. Bhattacharya believing the initiation of Asaṇga into Buddhist mysticism by Maitreyanath in Tusita heaven and his authoriship of Guhyasamāja Tantra apparently an early work on Buddhist Tantric doctrines suggests that Asaṇga was initiator of Tantra into Buddhism.[13] In support of his view he advocates Asaṇga as the protagonist of Prajñāpāramitā Sādhanā in Sādhanāmālā[14] Prof. A. B. Keith following the view of Prof. Levi believes the occurence of Tāntric rites in the early prajñāpāramitā doctrines of early Buddhism when he writes 'This illusion of Asaṇga reveals the existence in Buddhism of Tantric rites in which the Union of the Buddha and Bodhisattva with the personification of wisdom prajñapāramitā is reproduced on earth as one simple and effective mode of realising the true identity of the indivi dual with the Buddha.'[15] One comes across the word 'Parāvṛitti' in verses 41-46 in Chapter IX of Mahāyānasūtrālaṇkāra of Asaṇga. In these verses this prolific author of the Yogāchāra School of Mahāyāna narrates different kinds of parāvṛittis-Manasa parāvṛitti Sārthodgraha parāvṛitti, Vikalpa parāvṛitti, pratiṣthā parāvṛitti Maithuna parāvṛitti and Ākāśa-parāvṛitti to be practised by the adherents of Vijñānavāda for the realisation of Buddhahood.[16] As the whole narration of this work reveals parāvṛitti in this text is used in the sense of an ethical restraint on the different procliviteis of the perceptive and executive organs. Parāvṛitti as the persual of the whole work suggests signifies here as turning aside, restraint and abnegation and not as starting from a positive point to turn around to a negative or opposite point. Dr. Bagchi explains paravrittis of these verses as 'turning round to an opposite point' and to corroborate his view he argues that in the final stage of Buddhahood a Bodhisttva remains beyond all the false discriminations or Vikalpas of the mundane plane and parāvṛitti with regard to him does not mean abnegation but "enjoyment of bliss similar to that of sexual union."[16] A Asanga in chapter IX called Bodhyadhikāra in verse-7 of this work defines Buddhatva or Buddhahood as emancipation from all miseries all moral laxities and from the bondage of birth and death.[17] In this chapter in verse 14, he defines parivṛitti or parāvṛitti of Tathāgata as rising beyond all proclivites, refuge in āvṛitti or absolute cease of all proclivities and incessant repetition or uninterrupted continuity of Nivṛitti or abnegation of proclivities and Bibhutva as a result of incessant repetition or uninterrupted continuity of Nivritti or abnegation of proclivities.[18] In chapter XIX of this work this erudite scholar describes detachment towards enjoyments, sexual proclivities, strict adherence to a good and moral character and efficiencies in yoga as the fundamental virtues of a Bodhisattva and very clearly asserts that attachment to enjoyment, finding fault of other in an injurious way, pride, delicious taste of foods and evil and illusive mentation cause harms and hurdles on the way to perfection.[19]

The view of Prof. Tucci is subjected to serious doubts by several scholars. Prof. Chintaharan Chakravarty while corroborating the opinion of Prof. Tucci on the existence of a Soma Sect cites serious doubts on the doctrine of this Sect.[20] Mr. Nagendranath Upadhyaya considers the theory of Prof. Tucci as erroneous.[21] Prof. Winternitz.[22] also discards the view of Prof. Tucci who holds that Tantra arose in Buddhism as early as Fourth century A. D. Dr. Sahu also rejects the view of Prof. Tucci advocating that the restoration of the chinese word Na-ya-siu-mo as Soma School and identification of this Soma School as a sect of Śaiva Kāpālikas are subject to serioud doubts.[22A] As it has been suggested earlier Siddhānta as a doctrine and school of Śaivism appeared as early as the closing part of first century B. C.[23] The Siddhāntas incorporating the Somasiddhānta are the yogic schools of Śaivism and not the Tāntric School of Śaivism. Being a sub-sect of Śaiva school they profess beliefs in Śiva, Śakti, Shaṭchakrayoga or yoga based on six plexuses and even muttering of mantra but unlike the Tāntrists of Brāhmanical and Buddhist Tāntricisms they consider the killing of animals and contact with woman as the proscribed or prohibited actions of this sect. The view of Prof. Tucci really appears illogical. Dr. B. Bhattacharya conceives Asaṇga as the author of Śrī Guhyasamāja Tantra and assigns the time of Asaṇga as well as this Tantra to third century A. D.[24]

But his view fails to achieve recognition from a group of renowned critics. Prof. Winternitz places Asanga in the fourth century A. D. and Guhyasamāja Tantra in seventh century A. D.[25] He has also expressed a serious doubt on Asanga being a Tāntric author and the author of prajñāpāramitā Sādhanā or Sādhanā No. 159 in Sādhanāmālā[26] M. Anesaki places Asanga in fifth century A. D.[27] Prof Levi believes this Yogacharin author to have flourished in fifth century A. D.[28] Dr. S. Bagchi supporting the view of M. Anesaki believes Asaṇga as a man of fifth century A. D.[29] Dr. N. K. Sahu assigns the time of Asaṇga to fourth century A,D.[30] Prof A.L. Basham believes this Mahāyānist author as a Vijñānavādin of fifth century A.D.[31] Most of the illustrious scholars thus place Asanga either in fourth or in fifth century A.D. As Mr. N. N. Upadhyaya affirms, many scholars assign the date of Gujyasamāja Tantra to a period not prior to seventh century A. D.[32] According to his view Dr. Bhattacharya conceives Asaṇga as a Tantric author of third century A.D. and prajñāpāramitā Sādhanā in Sādhanāmālā and Guhyasamāja Tantra as the works of As aṇgasimply to prove this Vijñānavādin author as a Tāntric teacher of earlier days[33] Dr. S. Bagchi while refuting the view of Dr. Bhattacharya with regard to the author of Śrīguhyasamāja Tantra writes "Dr. Bhattacharya has tentatively suggested that Asanga who belonged to third century A.D. is the author of it. But this view cannot pass muster owing to the absence of its attestation by corroborative evidence.[34] Dr. Winternitz while rejecting Asaṇga as a Tāntric author also advocates that no where in the works of this Mahāyānist teacher which exist either in Tibetan or in Chinese translation that this teacher is illustrated to have learnt Tantra from Maitreyanāth in Tusita heaven.[35] Origin of Tantra in Buddhism became possible only when the esoteric school of Mantranaya or Mantrayāna arose in later Mahāyāna with a systematic concorporation of mantras or mystic incantation mudrā or mystic gesture and sexo-yogic partners, mandala or mystic diagrams, pañchakāmaguṇas or Pañchamakāras or Five Mas the doctrine of Śakti and .many other elements of proto-tāntric nature. These proto-Tāntric elements did not rush into Buddhism within a particular day or month or year but were shaped and systematised into a school of Mantranaya or Mantrayāna by a historical development of ages together[36] These elements being a heterogenous growth in Buddhism in several ages figured in large quantity in later Mahāyāna and it is probable that the protagonists of the Mahāyān-ist theology consociated with these elements systematised these elements into a Mantra School or Mantranaya or Mantrayāna. Organisation of this Mantranaya school by a group of later Mahayānists encouraged a schism in the Mahayāna of later days and Advayavajra, a Vajrayānist author recorded thus that Mahayāna is of two kinds—(A) Mantranaya and (B) Pāramitāna.[37] Mantranaya or Mantrayāna as various scholars suggest rightly was really the primary stage of Tantric Buddhism.[38] The Tibetan Tāntric Buddhist literature appears to suggest Mantranaya as the progenitor of Tantra in Buddhism when it classifies this Mantranaya into four tāntric parts-Kriyā Tantra, Charyā Tantra, Yoga Tantra and Anuttara yoga Tantra.[39] As it is rightly suggested by Dr. L.A. Waddell, about the end of Sixth century A.D. a large number of female energies in terrific and monstruous appearance were allotted as spouses to different celestial Buddhas and Bodhisttvas under the influence of Brāhmanical Tantras[40] and by the middle of seventh century A.D. Indian Buddhism having so many Buddhas and Bodhisattvas along with their spouses in terrific forms was introduced to Tibet,[41] The concept of Sakti was magnified in Brāhmanical Hinduism when the Devīmāhātmya section of Mārkaṇḍeya purāṇa was composed in sixth century A.D. and was interpolated to this purāṇa in that century.[42] According to J. N. Farquhar the period intervening between 500 A.D. to 900 A.D. is generally described as a Śākta period for during this period that Śāktaism in India attained a culminating as tendency and the works like puranas, Upapuranas, sectarian upanisads as also several earlier Tantras describing the magnanimity of Śakti were written with different Śāktaist doctrine.[43] Farquhar following the suggestion of Lāmā Tārānāth advocates the origin of Buddhist Tantra in 6th century A. D. As he writes in his own words—"Tārānath, the Tibetan historian says that the Buddhist Tantra was first written in Sixth century A. D. and he may well be right x x x x The Tathāgata gujyaka a perfect specimen of this class must belong to the first half of seventh century A. D. for it is quoted by Śāntideva in the middle of that century and the Tantra which Śubhakṛiṣhṇa, Vajrabodhi and his pupil Amoghavajra translated into chinese in the second decade of eighth century A. D. must belong to the first half of seventh atleast for Vajrabodhi died in his seventy first year in 772 A. D. and the name of his pupil contain the word Vajra which was a distinctive epithet of the new system.[44] The view of Farquhar seems to have carried a seed of truth atleast when he thesises that the Tantras translated by Śubhakṛiṣhṇa, Vajrabodhi and Amoghasiddhi in the second decade of eighth century A. D. must belong to later half of seventh century A. D. As Dr. N. Dutta suggests on the analysis of the chinese sources, Vajrabodhi and his pupil travelled to china in 719 A. D. and there they became the preceptors of Chen-yen school of chinese Buddhism, the theology of which is accompanied by esoteric elements.[45] Śubhakrishna who is rightly idnetified with Śubhākarasimha a king of Orissa brought to China Mahāvairochana Abhisaṁbodhi from Orissa.[46] Vajrabodhi, Amoghavajra and Śubhakṛiṣhṇa or Śubhākarasiṁha were all associated with the initial stage of Mantrayāna. Opinion of Farquhar lacks reasonability when he identifies Tathāgataguhyaka or Tathāgataguhyasūtra with Śrī Guhyasamāja Tantra, for none of the passages quoted in Śiksāsamuchchaya of Śāntideva from Tathāgataguhyaka occurs in Śrī Guhyasamāja Tantra.[47] Dr. Bagchi Dr. Winternitz and Dr. Sahu rightly consider Tathāgataguhyaka and Śrī Guhyasamāja Tantra as two different works,[48] Tathagataguhyaka called as Tāthāgata-guhyasūtra or Tathāgata Chintyā-guhyanirddeśa is a Mahāgāna Sūtra while Śrī Guhya samāja Tantra is a text of Vajrayāna. Tāntric elements are believed to have been interpolated into Mahāyānic text, Suvarnaprabhāsa sūtra in the early years of eight century A. D.[49] In view of the rise of Mantranaya in later Mahāyāna, Origin of Brāhmanical Tantras toward the close of sixth century A. D. influence of these Tantras on the conceptual growth of divine couples in later Mahāyāna and Mantranaya forms of Buddhism, congruence of most of scholars with regard to the transformation of several Mahāyānasutras and dhārṇīs into māntric formulaes during this period, consociation of Vajrabodhi, Amoghavajra and Śubhakṛishṇa with the initial organīsation of Mantranaya, interpolation of Tāntric elements into different Mahāyāna Sūtras like Suvarnaprabhāsa Sūtra by the beginning of eighth century and composition of Śrī Guhyasamaja Tantra presumably in 7th century A.D., it is plaucible to believe that Tantra originated in Buddhism from Seventh century A. D.[50] Prof. Winternitz Dr. Sahu and many others scholars are really the advocates of a right view when they assign the origin of this Tāntric Buddhism from seventh century A. D.[50A]

Mantranaya as revealed from Tibetan sources was originally preached in Dhānyakaṭaka.[51] Pandit Rahul Sankrityayana while inviting the attentions of scholars to a verse in Manjuśrīmūlakalpa identify Dhanyakaṭaka with Śrīparvata in Andhra.[52] Prof. L. A. Waddell basing his observation on Tibetan literature suggest the location of Dhānyakaṭaka in Kaliṇga.[53] He further affirms that this place of Kalinga had a famous Indian Tāntric monaslery and was a citadel of Kālachakrayāna.[54] The verse quoted by paundit Rahul Sankrityayana describes that all māntric Sādhanās performed in the great monutain Śrīparvata and Śrī dhānyakaṭaka in Dakṣhināpatha enable the adherents to achieve perfection or Siddhi quickly[55] Inviting the attention of scholars to an old Jaina text Jainakṣhetrasamāsa Mr. Nagendranath Vasu suggests the advent of pārśvanāth the twenty-third Tirthaṇkara to a place called Kopakaṭaka in Kaliṇga where he ended his fasting in the house of Dhanya a follower of Jainism.[56] After the end of this fasting Kopakaṭaka was also called as Dhānyakaṭaka which became a granary of paddy or Dhānya, [57] The author is inclined to identify this Kopakataka or Dhānyakaṭak with Kupari of Balasore district which as John Beams suggests had a Buddhist monastery and a Buddhist temple with a giagantic image of Buddha.[58] It is possible that the verse quoted by Paundit Rahul Sankrityayana refers Śrīparvata and Śrī Dhānyakaṭaka as two different places in Daksiṇāpatha both of which were the citadels of māntric Sādhanās. Kopakaṭaka probably figures as Kompāraka in parvatadroṇi in the copper plates of the Bhaumakara kings of Orissa and the Allahabad pillar Inscription of Samudragupta while referring to the conquest of several kingdoms in Dakshinapatha also describes the realms of Kośala Mahākāntār and Kaurala in Dakshiṇāpatha which are identified with the various regions of Orissa.[59] It is thus possible that Kuparī in Balasore was the Kopakaṭaka or Dhānyakaṭaka of the olden time and the motherland of Mantranaya school of Buddhism. In Saddharmapundarika-sutram Virajā the modern Jajpur is described as the land of the Padmaprabha Buddha and as the cradle land of Anuttar Bodhisattvayāna or Mahāyāna[60] Evidences from different sources also reveal that Mahayāna originated in Orissa[61] It is thus possible that Mantranaya or Mantrayāna originated in Orissa in Kopakaṭaka or Dhānyakaṭak or Kupari and was organised in Vajrayāna when Guhyasamāja Tantra was written after the organisation of the Tantric school of Guhyasamāja or secret conclaves for the realisation of the Vajra or Śunyatā nature of everything. The followers of Guhyasamāja aimed at the realisation of the vajra nature of Kaya, Vak and

Chitta in perfect comminglings[62] and Vajrasattva the supreme noumenon of Vajrayāna represented the unity of Kāya vajra, vākvajra and chitta vajra which are also described as Brahmā, Maheśvar and Viṣṇu—the Hindu Trinity—in Buddhist Tantra.[63] Indrabhuti, the vajrayānist king of Oḍḍiyāna invokes Vajrasattva as Jagannāth and Sāralā Dās the earliest known poet of the full-grown Oriya language analogises the holy triad of Jagannāth with the Hindu Trinity while depicting Lord Jagannath worshipped at Puri as Lord Buddha.[64] The Capital of the Bhaumakara kings of Tosala in Orissa was probably named Guhadeva pāṭaka or Guheśvara pāṭaka because the Bhauma kings were Buddhists and the Guhyasamāja aiming at the realisation of the Vajra nature of Kāya, Vāk and Chitta or Kāya Vajra Vāk vajra and Chhitta vajra evolved in Orissa. Guhyasamaja Tantra was introduced into Aryavartta from Oddiyana identified with Orissa, as it is suggested by Gos-lo-tsa-ba.[65]

Mantrayana was organised into Tāntric Buddhism in Oḍḍiyāna. Oḍḍiyāna or Uḍḍiyāna is described in pag-sam-jon-zang as the cradle land of Tānttic Buddhism.[66] Hevajra Tantra narrates four important pīṭhas as Jālandhara, Oḍḍiyāna, Purnagiri and Kāmarupa[68] Four piṭhas of Tāntric Buddhists depicted in Sādhanāmālā are K-āmakshya, Śirīhaṭṭa purnagiri and Uḍḍiyāna.[68] Among the four important Tāntric piṭhas described in Sādhanāmālā and Hevajra Tantra the two Tāntric Buddhist works, Oḍḍiyāna thus figures in both the texts and is depicted by pag-sam-jon-zang as the motherland of Tāntric Buddhism. Diametrically antithetical views prevail among the scholars with regard to the identity of Oḍḍiyāna. Prof. M. Sylvan Levi, Mr. F. W. Thomas, Mr. L. A. Waddell, Dr. P. C. Bagchi and Mr. S. C. Das, suggest the location of Oddiyana in Svat valley of Kabul[69] Mr. H. P. Sastri and following him Dr. B. Bhattacharya identify Oddiyana with Orissa[70] although in an another work Dr. Bhattacharya demostrates its location in Bengal[70]A Prof. Winternitz points out Oddiyana as Orissa of course not without a mark of in errogation[71] Dr. N. K. Sahu with a comprehensive discussion of several evidences identifies Oḍḍiyāna with Orissa[72] Mr. Nik Douglas considers Oḍra, Oḍḍiyāna and Orissa as identical terms and asserts the identity of Oḍḍiyāna with Orissa[73] Dr. K. C. Panigrahi justifies the identification of Oḍḍiyāna with Orissa on the basis of the latter's possession of huge Tāntric Buddhist remains[74] Dr. Thomas Eugene Donaldson citing evidences from several sources considers Uddiyana or Oddiyana as the variant of the words Oḍa, Oḍra, Uḍra, Oḍiviṣā and Oḍiyāna all of which according to his view refer to Orissa.[75] The Kālikā purāṇa while narrating the four tāntric piṭhas as Oḍra Jālaśhailaka, Purnapiṭha and Kāmarup in a resemblance with those of Hevajra Tantra an early Tāntric work of Buddhism records Oḍra in place of Oḍḍiyāna and affirms that Oḍra was the first and foremost piṭha among all.[76] Its description also asserts clearly that Goddess Kātyāyanī and Lord Jagannāth are the joint sovereigns of the Tāntric kingdom of Oḍra.[77] These descriptions are sufficient to prove that Oḍra was a variant of Oḍḍiyāna. The Yoginī Tantra while describing numerous Tāntric piṭhas and upapiṭhas narrates Oḍḍiyāna as the Tāntric piṭha of Krita age and all other Tāntric pithas as those of the later times.[78] The Tāntric piṭha Oddiyāna thus named with other variants like Uḍḍiyāna, Oḍa, Oḍra, Uḍra, Oḍiviṣā, Oḍicā and referring to Orissa also figures as Oḍrayāna in Sādhanāmālā a Tāntric Buddhist Text.

Scholars advocating the identity of Oḍḍiyāna with Swat valley generally depend on the phonetical similarity of a place called uḍyān in Svat valley on the doubtful intepretation of a paragraph from the acounts of Yuan Chhwang where Wu-tchang-na figures as a land of the people who are shy and crafty lover of learning practioner of the art of using charms and believers of Great Vehicle or Mahāyāna and geographical description of Oḍḍiyāna by Taranath and the author of Pag-sam-zon-zang[79] Dr. Sahu while examining the views of all these scholars has expressed a serious objection that the knowledges of Taranath, author of pag-sam-jon-zang and few Tibetan authors on the History and geography of India are open to serious doubt and that there is also the definite absence of the authentic clues in the works of Yuan chwann as to why the Tāntric land of Uḍḍiyāna will be identified with his Wu-tchang-na.[80] A comprehansive perusal of the different realible and relevant datas from various heterogenous sources by this author in one of his works however inculcates into his mind an impression that Oḍḍiyāna or Uḍḍiyāna of the Brāhmanical and Buddhist Tantra is probably no other than Orissa.[81]

Identification of Oḍḍiyāna or Uḍḍiyāna with swat valley appears quite illogical for various reasons. Although svat valley is very rich in preserving and possessing the antiquities of the earlier Gāndhāra school of arts, it does not display any where within its periphery the Tantric Buddhist antiquities of distinctive importance. Orissa is very rich in Tāntric Buddhist antiquities. In several Tāntric Buddhist texts Uḍḍiyāna is intimately associated with the adoration of Vajrasattva Tārā Marichī Kurukullā Lokeśvara, Padmapāṇī, Avalokiteśvara Vajravārāhī, Manjuśrī, Muchalinda Buddha, Vajrapāṇī, Trailokyavijaya and others[82]

The images of all these Tantric Buddhist deities are found in large numbers in Orissa in different places like Udayagiri, Lalitagiri, Ratnagiri, Kendrapara chowdvar, Banapur, Ganjam, Ayodhya, Khiching Jiunti, Nuagaon, Kantikula, Chaurasi, Khadipada, Jajpur, Astaranga, Talcher, Baud, Ghania-pali, near Bargarh, Binka, and many others. The Siddhas or the saints of Tāntric Buddhism have composed a large number of songs and dohas, the enthology of which being published by different scholars from Bengal, Orissa, Bihar and Assam is known variously as Bauddhagān O Dohā, Charyācharya Viniśchaya or Āścharya charyāchaya or Charyāgītikā or a name of the prototype in the interpretation and versions of the various scholars of Eastern India. The language of this enthology being typical Apabhramśa and really the parental source of various languages of Eastern India is claimed by a large number of scholars and linguists as old Oriyā, Old Beṇgalī Old Assāmese and old Maithilī.[83] All these scholars while claiming so have brought to a convincing illumination a consimilitude that really exists between idioms, syntax, vocables morphology, phonology and other linguistic and literary elements of these songs and Dohās of Tāntric Buddhism and those of the different languages of Eastern India. But no scholars have yet been known to have claimed the language of the charyā songs and dohās as the parental source of or in any way related with the language of Śvat valley. That Orissa was called Oḍḍiyāna in the ancient times is also testified by a number of South Indian inscriptions which record the term Oḍḍiyāna-galabai[84] These inscriptions belong to Fifteenth century A.D. Inviting a reference to the texts of Tibetan literature Dr. B. Bhattacharya advocates the opinion that Uḍḍiyāna as an extensive realm was consisting of two important kingdoms namely Sambhala and Laṇkāpuri and that the identification of Oḍḍiyāna by any scholar will not be construed valid until these two kingdoms are not properly and satisfactory identified[85] While displaying the unreasonable nature of the views of scholars who identify Laṇkāpuri with Swat valley on the conjecture that an immigrant tribe named Langga had migrated to this valley from various places of Beluchisthan,[86] who identify Laṇkā with Assam in consonance with a view of Prof. Jacobi, who incline to locate Rāmāyaṇic Laṇkā in Assam[87] and who identify Laṇkā as anologously as the Rāmāyanic Laṇkā in other parts of India[88] this author in one of his works believes reasonably that the Tāntric Buddhist Laṇkā is probably no other than Sonepur[89]

Sonepur figures as Paśchima Laṇkā or Western Lanka in the Sonepur copper plates[90] of Kumāra Someśvaradeva, a Somavaṁśī ruler and a perennial whirpool near a huge rock bed in river Mahānadi in Sonepur, which is called at present as lankeśvari Daraha is narrated as Laṇkāvarttaka in the Mahada copper place of Teluguchoda king Someśvaradeva II[91] Lankeśvari is narrated as a Tāntric Buddhist goddess in one of Sādhanās of the Tāntric Buddhist text Śādhanāmālā[92] in Tantric Buddhist iconographical text Niṣpannayogāvalī[93] and many other works. In Niṣpannayogāvalī, Lankeśvarī is described in association with Tāntric Buddhist deities Viramatī and Stambhakī which may be identified with the presiding Goddess Viramurchchā of Khaulgāḍ, or Khaul pit in Sonepnr and Stambheśvari worshipped in Sonepur, Kalahandi, Bolangir, Binka and many other localities of Western Orissā at least from the days of the king Tuṣtikara and queen Kaustubheśvarī in fifth century A. D.[94] The Sanepur Copper plates of Kumāra Śomeśvar and the Mahada copper plates of Teluguchoda ruler Someśvaradeva II are the records of eleventh century A. D. while Sādhanāmālā is placed in tenth-eleventh century A. D. and Niṣpannayogāvalī in 12th century A. D.[95] Dr. Bagchi without corroborating his view by sober evidences of history asserts conjecturally that Svat valley was related with the culture of Śrīchakrasambhara Tantra and its translator Jayadratha[96] The association of Sonepur with the culture of this Tantra, Jayadratha and the Tāntric rites of this Tantra carries a convincing reasonability for various reasons. In Niṣpanna-yogāvali of Paundit Abhayākaragupta, Lankeśvarī figures as deity in Samvara Maṇḍala of this text in Company of Śrīchakrasamvara Buddha, his consort Vojravārāhī and many other deities[97] Sonepur is even at present a citadel of the cult of Lankeśvarī and the antiquity of this cult of Lankeśvarī in Sonepur is sufficiently indicated by the inscriptional records of Orissa as early as eleventh century A.D. in their references to paśchima Laṇkā and Laṇkāvarttaka.[98]

The Kośaleśvara temple of Baidhyanāth carrying on the inscription "Daidi Dārikasyāpi" near its door suggests the cultural relation of Saha Jasiddha Dārikapāda with this place and temple[99] Dārikapāda originally named as Indrapāla and Vimalachandra was a[100] king of Kumārīkṣhetra, also called Kumārakṣhetra and Śāliputra in Tibetan source[101] This may rationally be identified with Kumārasimhā or Kumārīsimhā near Sonepur, and the antiquity of this Kumārasimhā may be dated back to Teluguchoḍa rule in eleventh century A.D. in Orissa on the basis of the Kumārīsimhā copper plate of the Teluguchoda king Somesvaradeva the grandson of Srimat chandradityadeva.[102] This Teluguchoda ruler Someśvaradeva records land-grant in village Kumārīsimhā in kumārīsimha copper plate.[103] There is also enough reason to believe that the Kośaleśvar temple was originally a Tāntric Buddhist shrine[104] Dārikapāda seems to be a petty ruler of Kumārsimhā in 9th century A.D. and became writer of so many works of Chakrasambhara Tantra Kālachakra Tantra and Vajrayoginī Tantra of Tāntric Buddhism soon after his initiation into Tāntric Buddhism[105] Jalendra the king of Tāntric Buddhist Laṇkā and father-in-law of Lakṣhmīṇkara embraced Tāntric Buddhism soon after he observed the Tāntric Siddhi of his daughter-in-law and was initiated into Tāntric Sādhanā of Vajravārāhī by one of his officer-saint who in turn was the Tāntric pupil of Lakṣhmīkarā[106] Vajravārāhī figures as the consort of Buddha Samvara in Niṣpanna Yogāvalī[107] The view of Dr. Bagchi is doubtlessly illogical because he does not cite any evidence, either on the intimate relationship of Svat valley with the culture of Śrīchakrasambhara Tantra or on the relationship of Jayadrath •with Svat valley. He also does not suggest any substantial evidence in favour of his identification of Laṇkā with Swat Valley. Langga as the name of a tribe can in no way explain satisfactorily the edentity of Laṇkā with Svat valley. Many •scholars identify Sambhala with Sambalpur of Orissa. Mr. B.C. Majumdar,[108] paundit Rahul

Sankrityayana[109] Dr. Karunakara Kara[110] Chandra Chakravartty[111] Dr. N.K. Sahu and many other scholars clearly write that Sambalpur was the ancient Sambhala or Sambalaka of Tāntric Buddhism.[112] A Buddhist Tantric text chaṇḍāmarichī Tantra ratnāvalī describes Sambalaka as a place on the bank of river Mahānadī, a place famous for the manufacture of diamond and a place of fame.[113] Such a place on the bank of the river Mahānadi can be no other than the ancient form of the modern Sambalpur. Odra probably signified a far-flung realm. Odra comprising Sarephahara Visaya figures in Soro copper places of Somadatta.[114] Sarephahara identified with Soro reasonable suggests that this part of Balasore was called Odra during the age of Somadatta. In Tekkali copper places of Śailodbhava king Madhyamarāja III Odra is described to have included the mountain Nasunda in its periphery.[115] Nasunda is identified with mount Nandavā near Tekkali in Ganjam district[116] It is probable that this part of Ganjam was called Odra during Śailodbhava rule. The uppalad copper plates of Rāṇaka Rāmadeva of Tailapa also narrates Nasunda as the crest-jewel of Oḍradesa.[117] In Baud copper plates of Raṇabhañjadeva lands are granted in favour of a Brahmin who was a resident of Bhāṭataralā in Oḍraviṣaya.[118] This Bhāṭataralā may be identified with Taralā in Ganjam. The Adipura charter of N-arendrabhañja narrates Odra with a village called Allaviḍraha[119] which may be identified with Ādinigarh in Baud phulvani district. The Brahmeśvara temple inscription of Kolāvatī devī delineates that Mahābhavagupta Janmejaya—I killed a king of Oḍra and fascinated his royal splendour[120] The king so killed was probably Raṇabhañja and Janmejaya having occupied Sonepur-Baud-Binka region made Sonepur the capital of his kingdom. Oḍra as a country and with village Kuḍukula in Gaṇḍitama Viṣaya is depicted in Orissa state Museum plates of Mahāśivagupta Yayati-I which was issued in fourth regnal year of this king from Binitapur[121] Kuḍukula in Gaṇḍitama Visaya may be identified with Karḍī near Gaḍmuṇḍā in Phulvani district and the donee of this grant as the original dweller of Kaṭaka may be accepted as a native of ancient puruṇākaṭak. Odra with Śilābhañjapāṭi figures in cuttack plates of Mahāśibagupta yayati—I which was issued from Binitapura[122] This Silābhanjapāṭi may be identified with Silati near Binka. All these illustrations thus make it clear that different parts of Orissa were called Oḍra, in different phases of time and it is probable that this common name was applied to different parts of Orissa because Oḍra, Oḍḍiyāna, Uḍḍiyāna, Oḍiviṣā and others variants were probably the general nomenclatures of Orissa at least in colloquial expression from a remote antiquity. The author feels that his view in this regard is not unreasonable when he observes that Sāralā Dās describes Orissa as Oḍrarāṣtra as early as fifteenth century A.D. and several south Indian inscription of this century while referring to Orissa name it as Oḍḍiyāna[123].

Vajrayāna, Sahajayāna and Kālachakrayāna thus constituting the three important schools of Tāntric Buddhism had originated in Oḍḍiyāna identified with Orissa. As Dr. B. Bhattacharya. Dr. N. K. Sahu and many other scholars write on the basis of Tibetan source an eye-catching number of scholars subscribing to the development of different original Tantras had flourished in Oḍḍiyāna.[124] Saraha, the propounder of Buddhakapāla Tantra and a founder advocate of Sahajayāna, Kambala and padmavajra, the pioneer of Hevajra Tantra. Luipāda the initiator of Sampuṭatilaka Tantra, Kukkurīpāda, the progenitor of Mahāmāyā Tantra, Lalitavajra the expounder of Kriṣhṇayamārī Tantra, Āchārya pitopāda the advocate of Śrīkālachakra Tantra, Gambhiravajra, the originator of Vajrāmṛita Tantra, Dārikapāda, a writer on chakrasambhara Tantra, Kālachakra Tantra and Vajrayoginī Tantra and many others were more or less consociated with Oḍḍiyāna which is identified with Orissa.[123] Padmavajra, Anangavajra and

Indrabhuti played vital role in the .initial organisation of Mantrayāna into Vajrayāna while Saraha in colloboration with Bhagavatī Lakṣhmīṇkarā the sister of King Indrabhuti and daughter-in-law of King Jalendra laid the foundation of a new school on the doctrines of Anuttara yoga tantra.[126] This new school was called Sahajayāna.-Āchārya pitopāda practised the esoteric yoga of Kālachakra Tantra in Sambhala, identified with Sombalpur and having systematised this Tantra into well-conceived doctrines and practices taught them in the monastic university of Ratnagiri in orissa called Oḍḍiyāna during his efflorescence as a Tāntric teacher[127] Padmavajra, a native of Oḍḍiyāna describes in his Guhyasiddhi, an authoritative work on Vajrayāna the doctrine and practices of this Tāntric Buddhist School in Sandhyā-bhāṣā or intentional language[128] This language was not a dialect of a particular region and was followed in many Tāntric and religious works of this age. It was really an enigmatic style of expression in which the writer tries to conceal the intended meaning from an Oridinary reader by the use of the words and phrases of many mean ings and leaves a clue simultaneously for the comprehensions of those devoted readers who really understand that secret doctrine of which he is a protagonist. As it is learnt from the accounts of Lāmā Tārānāth padmavajra in consociation with Kambalapāda introduced Hevajra Tantra into Buddhist Tāntric system. Anangavajra the author Prajñopāya Viniśchaya Siddhi describes Lord Jagannath as the preceptor of all and conferor of all siddhis.[129] Anaṇgavajra as known from his own work was a disciple of Śubhākara[130] who may be identified with Śubhakṛiṣhṇa or Śubhākarasiṁha a king of Orissa and the author of the mantrayanic work "Mahāvairochana abhisaṅ bodhi". This Subhākarasiṁha as it has been suggested earlier[131] played a Vital role in organising Mantrayāna or Mantranaya from later-Mahāyāna. Indrabhuti the vajrayānist king of Sambhala or Sambalaka in Oḍḍiyāna had his palace in Jatumati,[132] in Sambalaka. This Jatumati is identified with Jāmrā near Sambalpur and this author had been informed by many oldmen of Sambalpur that the ruins of an extensive stone plinth existed in Jāmrā region as late as the construction of the Dam of Hirakud. Indrabhuti as Dr. B. Bhattacharya rightly suggests was "an authority of Vajrayāna and Tantra" of Buddhism[133] and an author of a large number of works out of which twentythree texts are preserved in Tibetan bs-Tan-ghyur.[134] He is the author of Kurukullā Sādhanā collected in Sādhanāmālā[135] and of Jñānasiddhi[136] Dr. H. C. Das writes Indrabhuti as the author of Yajñasiddhi[137] but as no such work is assigned to the authorship of Indrabhuti it is probably mistaken for Jñānasiddhi by this learned scholar.[138] In Jñānasiddhi Indrabhuti and in prajñopāya Viniśchaya Siddhi his preceptor Anaṇgavajra narrate the primal Buddha of Tāntric Buddhism as Jagannāth and by many scholars this Buddha so named as Jagannāth is identified with Lord Jagannāth of Puri and many other temples in different parts of Orissa[139] Dr. K. C. Panigrahi interpretes Jagannāth of Jñānasiddhi purely in the literary meaning of this word and explaining it as the Lord of the Universe refutes the views of these scholars. But as a number of evidences from different sources of Buddhist and Brāhmanical Tantras and the religious texts of Orissa suggests the interrelation of this Orissan Jagannāth and Vajrasattva or Tāntric Buddhist Noumenon described in Jñānasiddhi of Indrabhuti and Prajñopāya-Viniśchayasiddhi of Jnaṇgavajra[140] it is reasonable indeed to believe that an identity had already been established between them during the Tāntric Buddhist age in Orissa. Indrabhuti is believed by this author to have emphasised the unique assimilative toleration of the cult of Lord Jagannāth by describing the God as 'Sarvajinavarāchitaṅ'[141] or "adorable by all those who have acquited command over their mundane proclivities" and the illusive mentation, Lakshmīṇkarā, the sister of the king Indrabhuti of Sambhala and the daughter-in-law of the kind Jalendra of Laṇkā was a leading female Tantrist of her age. She was the author of Advayasiddhi.[142] In collaboration with Saraha, the Ādi Siddha or the earliest founder-advocate of Sahajayāna, she organised initially this Tantric Buddhist school and promulgated in her work that the supreme truth can be realised by Anuttara yoga in the body and not by the physical torture, fasting, rites and ritual external purification of the body by bathing, nor by the observation of the rules and customs of the village religions, nor by the worship of images of the gods and goddesses made up of wood, stone and earth and not by any other religious formalities of the showing nature.[143] She also asserted that[144] all women irrespective of castes are the relative manifestation of Prajna and should not thus be abhorred under any circumstance. Padmasambhava the adopted son of the king Indrabhuti travelled to Tibet and became the founder of Lamaiṣm and also of the Sam-yas monastery.[145] Saraha the founder advocate of Sahajayana was born in Rājñī identified with Ranigarh near Jajpur in Orissa and was originally known as Rāhulabhadra.[146] As the Ādi Siddha of Sahajayāna he probably became efflorescent during the reign of the Bhaumakara king Śubhākaradeva I who ruled Tosala from his capital Guhyeśvarpāṭaka or Guhyadeva pāṭaka, a citadel for the Tāntric Sādhanas of the Guhyasamāja.[147] In Guhyasamāja Tantra Akṣhobhya is narrated to have initiated and established the Sarvatathāgata kāya-vāk-chitta Hṛidaya Vajra VIRAJASKA Mahāmaṇḍala for emnation of the five families of Vajrayāna.[148] The nomenclature Virajaska was probably assigned to this Mahāmaṇḍala probably because of its conceptual origin in Virajā, the antiquity of which may be dated back to the days of Indian epic Mahabharata.[149] Virajā is unquestionably identified with modern Jajpur. The Khadipada Image Inscription records the installation of the image of Padmapāṇī Avalokiteśvara by Mahāmṇdalāchārya paramaguru Rāhula ruchi.[150] As many scholars reasonably nourish a general credence this Rāhul aruchi is probably no other than Rāhul abhadra or Saraha, the founder-advocate of Sahajayāna. Luipāda described as a native of Oḍḍiyāna according to pag Sam-Jon-Zang[151] was a Kāyastha or scribe of the king Sāmantaśubha in Oḍḍiyāna[152] King Sāmanta-śubha may be identified with the king Śivānanda of N-andodbhava family who ruled in Airavata Mandala as a Vassal under the sovereignty of Bhaumakara[153] Talamula in Airāvata Maṇḍala is famous for Buddhist antiquities of Tāntric nature[154] Saraha is the author of a series of Tāntric Buddhist works and Luipada also[155] Sahajasiddas like Vajraghaṇṭapāda, Kambalapāda, virupā, kānhupāda, Dārikapāda, Sahajayoginī Chintā and many others are also related with Orissa in different ways. The Kālachakrayāna of Tāntric Buddhism is really a latest development in comparision with its two other sister-schools Vajrayāna and Sahajayāna. Prof. Agehananda Bharati without citing any substantial reason described Kālachakrayāna as of Non-Indian origin[156] But as a lot of evidences are traced out with regard to the doctrinal evolution of Kāla as Paramatattva or Supreme Reality in several Indian texts of astrological and religious nature, as the profound influence of astrology are clearly observed on the doctorines and rituals of Kālachakra Tantra, as in Tibetan literature there is sufficient indication of Sambala as the cradle land of Kālachakrayāna and as testimonies from different sources suggest Orissa as the citadel of this Tāntric school, it is reasonable to believe that this school of Tāntric Buddhism is of Indian Origin[157] According to Lāmā Tārānāth, Āchārya Pitopāda was sent by Bodhisattva Vajrapāṇī for the acquisition of Knowledge in different Tantras.[158] It is also suggested that this Achārya brought from Sambhala many Tantras with him and taught them to his students in Monastic university of Ratnagiri[159] Āchārya Pitopāda is famous for having introduced Kālachakratantra with a proper systematisation into Tāntric Buddhism. This Āchārya appears to have flourished as a Tāntric teacher of Ratnagiri probably in 10th century A. D.[160] In a manuscript entitled Laghukālachakra tantra-rāja Tikā or Vimalaprabhā which had been copied by one palm-leaf writer during the reign of the king Harivarmandeve of Varman dynasty of East Bengal[161] Mr. B. Bandopadhyaya traces out the name of one Yaśorāja the king of Sambhala as a devoted patron of Kālachakrayāna[162] This Yaśorāja of Vimalaprabhā may be identified with the Teluguchoḍa King Yaśorājadeva-I who carved out a dominion in South Kośala as early as 1070 A. D. under the overlordship of the Chindakanāga king Some śvaradeva of Chakrakoṭa Maṇḍala[163]

All these discussion thus make it plausible ȷo believe that Vajrayāna, Sahajayāna an Kālachakrayāna Originated in Oḍḍiyāna identified with Orissa and from Orissa they travelled to different parts of India and even abroad in Tantric missions of different preachers like Śubhākarasiṁha, padmasambhava and many others.

REFERENCES

1. Dr. S. B. Dasgupta—An Introduction to Tāntric Buddhism (University of Calcutta 1974) p. 2. Ed. H. Bhattacharya—The cultural Heritage of India Vol. IV. (Ramakrishna Mission Calcutta 1969) p. 211. (view of Dr. P.C. Bagchi in Evolution of the Tantras) Dr. N. K. Sahu Buddhism in Orissa pp. 122-127. Prof. C. Chakravatti-Tantras, studies on their religion and literature (Punthi Pustak, Calcutta 1963) pp. 1-20. Dr. D. N. Bose—Tantra-their philosophy and occult secrets (Calcutta) p. 1-25. Tsong-Ka-pa-Tantra in Tibet (George Allen and Unwin Ltd. London 1977) Chap-I and II etc. etc.
2. Dr. R. P. Mishra—Sahajayāna—A study of Tāntric Buddhism (Punthi Pustak, Calcutta 1991) pp. 28-29.
3. F. D. Lessing and A. Waymann—Introduction to the Buddhist Tāntric system (Motilal Banarsidass 1978) pp. 100-101.
4. Dr. N. K. Sahu—Buddhism in Orissa. p. 131.
5. Dr. S. B. Dasgupta—obscure Religious cults (Firma KLM Private Limited Calcutta 1976) p. 24. Also An Introduction to Tantric Buddhism (University of Calcutta 1974) p. 63.
6. Ed. Dr. S. Bagchi-Śrīguhyasamāja Tantram (Mithila Institute Dharbhanga 1965). p. 125 Chap-XVIII verse 51.
   Guhyasiddhi (M. S. C. L. B. No. 3/24) p. 6A.
   Hevjara Tantra (M. S. R. A. S. B. No. 11317). pp. 2A-5a.
   Dr. S. B. Dasgupta—An Introduction to Tāntric Buddhism pp. 62-63, 70-74, 77-78, 81-82 etc.
7. Dr. R. P. Mishra—Sahajayāna—A study of Tāntric Buddhism. pp. 29-30 M. Sylvan Levi Translation of Mahāyāna Sūtrālaṇkāra Journal of Asiatic Society of Bengal (N. S.) Vol. XXVI. 1930 pp. 129-130 Ed. Dr. B. Bhattacharya Śrī Guhyasamāja Tantram (GOS Baroda) Preface and Introduction, P. XIX and XXXII. Sadhanamala Vol-II, p. XXVIII. An Introduction to Buddhist Esoterism. pp. 54 and 62, A, B. Keith-Buddhist Philosophy. p. 301.
8. Prof. M. Sylvan Levi—Translation of Mahāyānatūtralankara. p. 81.
9. Dr. N. K. Sahu—Buddhism in Orissa pp. 123-127. Dr. R.P. Mishra —Sahajayāna—A Study of Tantric Buddhism. pp. 29-30. Dr. P. C. Bagchi studies in Tantra. P-I. p. 92 (Calcutta University, Calcutta 1939).
10. J. A. S. B (NS) Vol. XXVI 1930. pp. 129-130.
11. Ibid.

12. Ibid.
13. Dr. B. Bhattacharya—Guhyasamāja Tantra Intro p. XIX. and XXXII Sādhanāmālā Vol. II. Intro. p. XXVIII. An Introduction to Buddhist Esoterism. pp 54 and 62.
14. Ibid.
15. A. B. Keith—Buddhist Philosophy (Oxford) p. 301.
16. Ed. Dr. S. Bagchi—Mahayana Sutralankara of Asanga (Mithila Institute Darbhanga 1970). pp. 43-44. Chap—IX verses 41-46.
16A. Dr. P. C. Bagchi Studies in Tantra p. 92.
17. and
18. Ed. S. Bagchi—Mahāyāna Sūtrālaṇkāra—p. 38. Chap. IX verse-7 p. 39. chap—IX verse 14.
19. Ibid. pp. 157-158. Chap XIX. verse 24 and 30. 31-33.
20. Indian Historical quarter. Vol. VIII. p. 221ff.
21. Mr. N. N. Upadhyaya—Tāntric Bauddha Sādhanā Aur *S*āhitra (Nagari Pracharini Sabha Kashi). pp. 92-93. (Samvat 2015).
22. M. Winternitz—A history of Indian Literature, Vol. II. (Munsiram Manoharlal New Delhi 1972). p. 634.
22A. Dr. N. K. Sahu—Buddhism in Orissa p. 125.
23. Dr. S. N. Dasgupta—A history of Indian Philosophy (Motilal Banarsidass 1975). p. 70.
24. Ed. B. Bhattachary—Guhyasamāja Tantra Intro XI—XII, XXXII, XXXIV.
25. and
26. M Winternitz—A history of Indian Literature of Vol. II. pp. 355-356, 394 and also page 392.
27. M. Anesaki—Encylopaedia of Religion and Ethics. Vol. II. p. 62.
28. Ed. S. Bagchi—Mahayāna Sūtrālaṇkāra Intro. p. 6.
29. Ibid—Introduction. p. 5-6.
30. Dr. N. K. Sahu—Buddhism in Orissa, p. 124.
31. Prof. A. L. Basham—The wonder that was India (Sidwick and Jackson London (Reprinted 1985). pp. 279-281.
32. Mr. N. N. Upadhyaya—Tāntric Bauddha Sādhanā Aur Sāhitya p. 91.
33. Ibid.
34. Ed. S. Bagchi—Śrighuhyasamāja Tantram Intro. p. II.
35. M. Winternitz's view in Indian Historical quarterly IX, March 1933. pp. 5-6. Dr. R. P. Mishra—Sahajayāna—A study of Tāntric Buddhism. p. 31 and p. 87 foot note No. 36.

36. Dr. R. P. Mishra—Sahajayāna—A study of Tāntric Buddhism. pp. 28-84.
37. Ed. H. P. Sastri—Advaya Vajrasamgraha (GOS XL 1927) p. 14. Baroda.
38. Dr. S. B. Dasgupta—An introduction to Tāntric Buddhism. 52-53. Dr. N. K. Sahu—Buddhism in Orissa. pp. 128-131.
39. F. D. Lessing and A Wayman—An introduction to Buddhist Tāntric system. pp. 100-101.
40. L. A. Waddell—Tibetan Buddhism (Dover publication Inc. New and yord 1972). p. 14.
41.
42. Dr. M. Winternitz—A history of Indian Literature Vol. I, (Munsiram Manoharlal New Delhi 1972). p. 565.
43. J. N. Farquhar—An outline of the religious literature of India (Oxford 1920). p. 200 Prof. C. Chakravartty—The Tantras—Studies on their Religious and literature. p. 19.
44. J. N. Farquhar—An outline of Religious Literature of India pp. 210-211.
45. Ed. S. Radhakrishnan and others—The cultural Heritage of India Vol. I. p. 497.
46. M. Winternitz—A history of Indian Literature Vol. II. p. 400 F. N. No. 4.
47. Ibid, p. 635.
48. Dr. Bagchi—Śrī Guhyasamāja Tantra Intro. p. II. F. N. No. 1. Dr. N. K. Sahu—Buddhism in Orissa. p. 126.
49. Ed. S. Bagchi—Suvarnaprabhāsa sūtram (Mithila Institute Darbhanga 1967) Intro. pp. 1. 18.
50. Dr. R. P. Mishra—Sahajayāna—A study of Tāntric Buddhism pp. 29-41.

51A. M. Winternitz—Indian Historical quarterly Vol. IX. p. 8. (1933). Dr. N. K. Sahu—Buddhism in Orissa p. 127.

51. E. M. Dargyay—The Rise of Esoteric Buddhism in Tibet (Motilal Banarsidass New Delhi 1977). p. 16.
52. "Śrīparvate Mahāśaile Dakṣhināpatha Saṁjnike Śrī Dhānyakaṭake Chaitye Jinadātudhare Bhuvi Siddhyanti Tantra mantra Vai Kshipram Sarvārtha Karmasu".
53. L. A. Waddell—Tibetan Buddhism. pp. 268-269.
54. Ibid, pp. 268-269.
    Orissa History congress procedings XII Jyotivihar 1986. pp. 10-17
55. See Foot note No. 52 of this article.

56. N. N. Vasu—Archaeological survey of Mayurbhanja. p. XLIV Dr. H. C. Das—Cultural Development in Orissa. (Punthi Pustak Calcutta 1983). p. 203.
57. Ibid.
58. Dr. H. C. Das—Cultural Development in Orissa. p. 162.
59. Pt. B. Mishra—Orissa Under the Bhauma kinga. p. 3. Dr. B. Das—The Bhaumakaras—Buddhist kings of Orissa and their times (Oriental Publisher New Delhi 1978). p. 90.
60. Ed. P. L. Vaidya—Saddharmapuṇḍarikasūtram (Mithila Institute Darbhanga 1960). p. 48. chap. III. Oupamya Parivattah—Line 3-4. Line II. see also p. 49. verse 25 of this chapter Dr. R. P. Mishra—Sahajayāna—A study of Tantric Buddhism. p. 9. and p. 21. Foot note No. 73 and 74 See also Koṇārka—Oḍiśhā Sahitya Akademi Bhubaneṣvar. Vol. 68. 1988 pp. 11-21 See the Essay Odishare Mahayana.
61. Konarka—Orissa Sahitya Akademi Bhubanesvar. Vol. 68 1988. pp. 11-21. Dr. N. K. Sahu—Buddhism in Orissa. pp. 68 71.
62. and
63. Śrī Guhyasamāja Tantra Ed. by Dr. S. Bagchi p. 105. Chap XVII verse 19. see also the whole chap I of this text.
64. Ed. B Bhattacharya—Two Vajrayāna works-Jñānasiddi, Chap I, verse I, chap. I verse 92. chap. II, verse 28 and chap IV, verse 8. Dr. R. P. Mishra—Sahajayāna—A study of Tāntric Buddhism pp. 43-44 and p. 95 foot note No. 157 and 158.
65. G. N. Reerich—The Blue Annals, Vol. I (Calcutta 1949), p. 361 ff.
66. Dr. B. Bhattacharya—Sādhanāmālā, Vol. II. Intro p. XXXVII. An Introduction to Buddhist Esoterism. p. 45. Dr. N. K. Sahu—Buddhism in Orissa. p. 142. Dr. R. P. Mishra—Sahajayāna—A study of Tāntric Buddhism, p. 41.
67. Ed. D. L. Snellgrove—The Hevajra Tantra. Vol. I (Oxford 1959) p. 14f.
68. Ed. B. Bhattacharya—Sādhanāmālā Vol. II. pp. 453-455.
69. View of S. Levi in Journal Asiatique 1915 p.105. ff. view of Thomsa in Journal Asiatique society 1906. p. 461. L. A. Waddell—Tibetan Buddhism. p. 26. Indian Historical quarterly VI. p. 576 ff. B. Bhattacharya—An introduction to Buddhist Esoterism. p. 44 (view of Das cited).
70. B. Bhattacharya—Sādhanāmālā Part—II Intro p. XXXVII Indian. Buddhist Iconography—Intro. XXVII.

70A. B. Bhattacharya—An Introduction to Buddhist Esoterism (C. S. S. O. Baranasi 1964) pp. 43-46.

71. M. Winternitz—A history of Indian Literature, Vol. II. p. 393.
72. Dr. N. K. Sahu Buddhism in Orissa. pp. 141-152.
73. N. Douglas—Tantrayoga (Munsiram Manoharlal New Delhi 1982) pp. 6-7.
74. Dr. K, C. Panigrahi—History of Orissa (Kitab Mahal Cuttack) 1981 p. 309.
75. Ed, P. Tarkaratna—Kālikpurāṇa (Bangavasi Edition Calcutta) Chap. 64. p. 410 Dr. R. P. Mishra—Sahajayāna—A study of Tāntric Buddhism p. 43.
77. Ibid (both).
78. Pt. K. L. Mishra—Yoginī Tantra (Lakshmi Venkatesvar Press Kalyan Bombay Samvat 2013 Sakabda 1878) p. 240. Uttarakanda Prathamapatala verses 5-60.
79. Dr. R. P. Mishra—Sahajayāna—A study of Tāntric Buddhism pp. 41-42. Dr. N.K. sahu-Buddhism in Orissa pp. 142-144 and p.152.
80. Dr. N. K. Sahu—Buddhism in Orissa p. 152,
81. Dr. R. P. Mishra—Sahajayāna—A history of Tāntric Buddhism pp. 41-42. Dr. N. K, Sahu—Buddhism in Orissa. pp. 142-144 and p. 152.
82. Ibid—Chapter VII. pp. 346-352, Dr. N, K. Sahu—Buddhism in Orissa pp. 181-200.
83. Dr. R. P. Mishra—Sahajayāna—A study of Tāntric Buddhism. p. 333-334.
84. Dr. R. Subrahmanyam—The Suryavaṁśī Gajapatis of Orissa (Andhra University Waltair 1957), p.46 and also foot note No.67 of
85. the page Dr. B. Bhattacharya—An introduction to Buddhist Esoterism pp. 44-46.
86. Dr. R. P. Mishra-Sahajayāna—A study of Tāntric Buddhism pp. 53-55.

87,
88. and
89.

90. Dr. S. N. Rajaguru—Inscriptions of Orissa Vol. IV. p. 269. Epigraphia Indica. Vol. XII. pp. 237-242. Epigraphis Indica Vol. XXVIII. pp, 321-326.
91, Epigraphic Indica Vol. XXVIII. p. 283f. Dr. N. K. Sahu—Utkal University. History of Orissa Vol. I. (1964 Edition). pp. 138-139.
92. Ed. B. Bhattacharya—Sādhanāmalā. p. II. Sadhana No. 218. p.427.
93. Ed. B. Bhattacharya—Niṣpannayogāvalī (G. O. S. Baroda No. 109) 1972. p. 79.
94. Epigraphia Indica Vol. XXX. pp. 274-278ff Terasing a plates of King Tushtikara.

95. Dr. R.P. Mishra Sahajayāna—A study of Tāntric Buddhism. p. 52.
96. Indian Historical quarterly. Vol. VI. p. 583.
97. Ed. B. Bhattacharya—Niṣpannayogāvali. pp. 26-27.
98. See foot notes No. 90 and 91 of this article.
99. Sri S. Agrawala—Sonepur Itihāsa Part. I (Atmaprakasani Bolangir 1988). 11.
100. Bibliotheca Indo—Tibetica (4) The Biography of Eighty four saints by Abhayadatta Sri Editted By sempa Dorje (Central Institute of Higher Tibetan studies Sarnath Varanasi 1979). p. 140 also foot note No. 2 of this page.
101. Ibid.
102. Kumarisimha copper plate of Teluguchoda king some svaradeva II in Journal of Kalinga Historical Research society. Vol. I. No. 1. see lines 10-11 of this Inscription.
103. Ibid.
104. Charles Louis Fabri-Art of Orissa (Orient Longman Bombay) p. 30.
105. Ed. B. Bhattacharya—An introductien of Buddhist Esoterism. p. 78.
106. Ed. Sempa Dorje—The Biography of Eighty four sanits by Abhadatta Sri pp. 150-151.
107. Ed. B. Bhattacharya—Nispanna Yogavali. p. 26.
108. B C. Majumdar—Orissa in the making (Calcutta 1925). pp. 77-79.
109. Pt. R. Sankrityayana—Journal Asiatique Paris CC XXV 1934. p. 209.
110. Dr. Karuna Kara Kara—Āścharya Charyā Caya, pp. 10-11. (Orissa Sahitya Akademi 1969) Bhubanesvar.
111. C. Chakravartty—Sex life in Ancient India (Firma KLM Calcutta 1963). pp. 93-94.
112. Dr. N. K. Sahu—Buddhism in Orissa. pp. 147-150.
113. Dr. R. P. Mishra-Sahajayāna—A study of Tāntric Buddhism p. 46.
114. Epigraphia Indica. Vol. XXIII. p. 202.
S.N. Rajaguru—Inscriptions of Orissa, Vol. I. Part II.(Berhampur 1958). No. 29. p. 138-139.
115. S. N. Rajaguru—Inscriptions of Orissa Vol. I. Part II. No. 46. p. 243. Line 18.
116. Ibid. p. 246 Journal of Andhra Historical Research society. Vol. X. p. 166.
117. Journal of Andhra Historical Research society. Vol, IX. 1936-1937, p. 166.

S. N. Rajaguru—Oḍishāra Itihāsa-Grantha Mandira, Cuttack 1985. p. 267.

118. S Tripthy—Inscriptions of Orissa. Vol. VI (Sarada Press Bhubaneswar 1974). pp, 21-23.
119. Indian Historical quarterly, Vol. X. pp. 473-477.
120. Journal of Asiatic society of Bengal. Vol. VII. June 1837. pp. 557-562 ff. verse 2 of this inscription.
121. S. N. Rajaguru—Inscriptions of Orissa. Vol. IV. No. 26. pp. 159-163.
122. Epigraphia, Indica Vol. III, pp. 351-355.
123. Sāralā Mahābhārata-Virātaparva 'Jambudvipa Bharatakhanda Mandala Oḍra-rāṣṭre' Dr. R. Subramanyam—The Suryavaṁśī Gajapati of Orissa. p. 46.
124. Dr. N. K. Sahu—Buddhism in Orissa. p. 142.
125. Ibid.

    Dr. B. Bhattacharya—An Introduction to Buddhist Esoterism p. 78.
126. Dr. N. K. Sahu—Buddhism in Orissa. pp. 162-172,

    Dr. R. P. Mishra—Sahajayāna—A study of Tāntric Buddhism. pp. 28-83.
127. Orissa History congress proceedings XII Annual session Jyotivihar 1986. pp. 10-17.
128. Dr. B. Bhattacharya—An Introduction to Buddhist Esoterism.
129. p. 70. Dr. K. K. Kara—Āścharyacharyāchaya, p. 15. Prajnopāya Viniśchaya Siddhi quoted.
130. Ibid.
131. See above in this article.
132. L. A. Waddell. Tibetan Buddhism, pp. 380-381.
133. Ed. B. Bhattacharya—An Introduction to Buddhism. pp. 74-75.
134. Ibid.
135. Ibid.
136. Ibid.
137. Dr. H.C. Das. Cultural Development in Orissa. pp. 145, 147, 369.
138. Ed. Dr. B. Bhattacharya-Two vajrayāna works (G. O. S. Baroda 1929. See Jnānasiddhi whole work and preface.
139. Dr. K. K. Kara-Āścharyacharyāchaya. pp. 13-15. Dr. N. K. Sahu Buddhism in Orissa. pp. 145-146.
140. See Notes No. 129 and 64 of this article.
141. Ed. B. Bhattacharya—Two Vajrayāna works-Jnanasiddhi chapter-I. verse I.

142. Ed. M. J. Shendge—Advayasiddhi of Lakshmīṇkarā (G. O. S. Baroda, Feb. 1964).
143. Ibid. verses 13-14.
144. Ibid. verse 21.
145. L. A. Waddell-Tibetan Buddhism. pp. 24-28.
146. Dr. R. P. Mishra—Sahajayāna—A study of Tāntric Buddhism. pp. 117-118.
147. Ibid. pp. 117-121.
148. Ed. S. Bagchi-Śrīguhyasamāja Tantra. p-2 Chapter-I.
149. Konarka-Orissa Sahitya Akademi, Volume 68 (1988 Bhubaneswar, pp. 20 and 27, foot note No. 60.
150. Dr. R. P. Mishra-Sahajayāna—A study of Tāntric Buddhishm. p-38. Epigraphic Indica. Vol-XXVI. pp. 247ff proceedings of Indian History congress XII, session (1949). pp. 66-67.
151. Dr. Sumpa Khan-Pāg-sām-jon-zāng-Index p. CXIV.
152. Dr. N. K. Sahu-Buddhism in Orissa. p. 164. Ed. B. Bhattacharya. An Introduction to Buddhism Esoterism. p-69.
153. Dr. R. P. Mishra Sahajayāna—A study of Tāntric Buddhism p. 122-123.
154. Ibid.
155. Ibid. pp. 119-123.
156. Prof. A. Bharati-The Tantric Tradition (B. I. Publication New Delhi 1976) p. 222.
157. Orissa History congress procedings XII Annual session Jyoti Vihar, Burla 1986. pp. 10-20. Dr. R. P. Mishra-Sahajayāna—A study of Tāntric Buddhism pp. 76-83.
158. B. N. Dutta-Mystic tales of Lāmā Tārānāth (Ramakrishna Vedanta Matha Calcutta 1944)· p-49.
159. Orissa History congress proceedings XII Annual session Jyoti Vihar, Burla 1986. pp. 10-17.
160. Ibid.
161. Journal of Asiatic Society letters. Vol-XVIII. No. 2. 1952. pp. 74-75. Dr. R. P. Mishra-Sahajayāna—A Study of Tāntric Buddhism pp. 46-50.
162. Ibid.
163. Ibid.

Orissa History congress proceedings XII Annual session Jyoti Vihar, Burla 1986. pp. 16-17.

BHAKTIMOVEMENT AND FOLK-INSTITUTIONS

5

3

BHAKTIMOVEMENT AND FOLK-INSTITUTIONS

Dr. Dolagobinda Bishi
Principal P. S. College, Saintala

The Role of 'Dharma' is most essential to reform mankind and the society. The exterior of 'Dharma' has come under the influence of different ideologies and reforms during the different phases of history, but its innerself or the soul has remained unchanged. The core of Dharma is Bhakti.

Ever since the onset of Indian civilization Bhakti movement has all along been one of the fundamental characteristics of its culture. For centuries together this eternal thought has been propagated by the Indian Saints and asceties for the welfare of humanity through scripture and literature. The Principle of 'Basudhaiva Kuṭumbakaṁ' finds its genesis in Bhakti cult. The Bhakti cult has been growing and expanding without interruption and dilution through the medium of multi-religious views and sects ever since the Vedic times to contemporary period. The historians have divided Bhakti movement into three Renaissance periods. The first renaissance is from 1500 B. C. to 500 B. C. Scholars mention about the Śāswat Pañchrātra and Bhagat Bhakti during the phase. The Second renaissance continued from 700 A. D. to 1400 A. D. and scholars point out about the Bhakti of Alwar devotees and Āchāryas of this period. The third renaissance was from 1400 A. D. to 1900 A. D. This period is known as the true popular movement of Bhakti Movement. During this time many Bhakti based folk institutions and propaganda based Bhakti literature flourished. But primarily the period from 12th century to 16th century or the mediaval cultural movement period has been defined as the Bhakti movement period by scholars. Truly this Neo-Bhakti movement based on the principle of humanistic Baiṣhṇabi Philosophy paved the way for the establishment of a non-discriminating, pure and an intergrated social order ; by creating an atmosphere of social equality irrespective of race, religion, caste and creed, giving rise to a social renaissance, unity, human integration and a reformative social milieu which was able to preserve the Eternity (Sanātanatā) of Hindu culture. In reality, this cultural movement inter-relating God, universe and salvation was a all pervasive national movement. During that time in no part of the country no individual was there who was left untouched by this reformative socio-nationalist movement. After the Vedic age this period was truly the Golden age in the cultural history of India. From time to time there might have been changes in the political spheres, but from cultural point of view this nation was one as proved by the Bhakti Movement.

The pioneers and activists of Bhaktimovement were primarily creative religious poets and Saints. They propagated their humanistic philosophy in the society in the form of literature and lyrics and which transformed the Bhakti movement into a treasure for the people in general. As a result of which this Bhaktimovement, with the support of folk culture was greatly propagated in the society by different folk institutions. Due to its influence and its propagation many new folk institutions came into existence and by means of folk songs, folk dance, and folk drama Bhakti movement was glorified and at the same time Bhakti literature came to be propagated.

The Folk institutions accepted the Bhakti movement with ease due to the fact that both the Bhakti movement and folk centres had aims of achieving social equality and a spirit of unity irrespective of religion, Caste and creed. As a result,

Bhakti movement through the medium of folk-institutions became popular. The origination of folk-institution like "Pāiā" in Orissa as a result of the blending of Hindu Bhakti cult and Islamic suffism became remarkable in the context of National unity. The Bhakti consciousness of the people gave birth to all the religious fairs, festivals, temples and like institutions every where in India.

Fairs, Festivals and Devotional thought go together The Spokesmen of Brahminism differentiated between Caste, creed and religion on the basis of God, whereas the propagators of humanistic Bhakti cult emphasised the medium of fairs and festivals which could unite different caste, creed and religion on the same basis of God. From this point, the Kumbhamelā, the Makaramelā, the Śivarāti Melā, Dola yātrā, Chandan yātra, Jhāmu Yātrā, Ratha yātrā, held in various parts of India are noteworthy. Writing on the various religious festivals of South India a scholar has noted "The Characteri stics of Hindu Festivals find an echo in some of the Christian and Muslim festivals also". This is a fine example of National Integration especially in all the fairs and festivals held in South India where the theme of Service to mankind occupies the most prominent position, during the festival period, religious discourses, devotional recitals by Thevaram and Prabandam singers in groups are performed to seek the glorification of Bhakti and God.

The humanistic philosophy and Bhakti consciousness in the back ground of fairs and festivals eulogises God and the devotees irrespective of their caste, creed colour and religion by bringing the deities from inside the temples for a closer affinity with the general people. In the context the example of the Car festival of Lord Jagannāth in Puri of Orissa and Theruvoram temple of Tamilnadu is very remarkable. By ignoring all the blind and puritantic laws of Brahminism thousands of devotees irrespective of their caste and creed pull the Ratha of the Lord. Today the car festival of Puri is world famous as the greatest even of all pervesive Bhakticult.

These fairs and festivals are only Folk-institutions created by the saints and asceties. But, it is a matter of regret that for the analysis of Bhakti movement and the role of folk-institutions no proper research has yet been conducted by scholars. The debate and discussions of the scholars has been resticted only to the creative literature of saints and suffists. Moreover, in the present time also numerous folk institutions continue to profess and propagate the Bhakti cult throughout the country, for instance, the 'Krishnaguru Bhajan' of the Western Orissa.

ROLE OF SANKIRTAN :

In the history of Bhakti movement the folk institutions symbolising Indian culture and value occupy a very important place. In this context the 'Mahimā' of Kirtan is known to every-body. Saṇkirtan is the easiest and most popular medium of Bhakti movement. The rale of Saṇkirtana has taken the important position in India. All the devotees and saints of Bhakti age have propagated their sayings, couplets, and songs throuth the Sankirtan. This folk institutions can truly be called as the true catalyst of Bhakti movement. Baishnaba Acharyas have given importance to Kirtan in Nabadhā Bhakti. The concept Kirtan includes both Bhakti and Bhakta. In popular sense to recite the glory of God through devotional music in a loud voice is Kirtan. The Bhaktas consider kirtan as worship of 'Sākāra Śabda Brahma', At first Debarṣhi Nārada started this best medium of Bhakti. In the Tretayā Age, Rām Bhakta Hanumān popularised this tradition throuth the Rām-Nām-Kirtan.

Not a single devotee and saint in Kali Yug can be found

who has not taken recourse to the Folk-institution sankirtan to propagate his views and Bhakti movement.

In the History of Hindi literature Bhakti period (1318 A. D. to 1643 A. D) is known as the golden period. Truly, Hindi literature of this period is nothing but kirtan literature. That is why in the history of Hindi literature Santh Kabir Das, Bhaktabara Sur Das, Goswami Tulsi Das Mirabai, Santh Rai Das, Rahim, Khankhana, Bhakta Raskhan, Kumbhan Das, Krushna Das, Paramananda Das, Krushna Das (2) Balak Chatrubhuj Das, Nanda Das, Gondiswamy, Chitswamy, Chaturbhuja Das (2) Dadu Γayal, Maluk Das, Nagari Das, Sri Bhattaji, Lalit Kishori, Sahajo Bai, Rasik Bihari, Jugal Priya Rani Roop Kumari, Yaari, Sahib, Tajbi, Daria Saheb, can be identified as Kirtankār poets. Spokesman of Bhakti cult and the first Guru of Sikha Śrī Nānak Dev was a devout saint and kirtan lover. Now also in gurudwāras and temples the sayings of Nānak Dev comlpiled in the "Guru Granta Saheb" are sung through saṇkirtan.

All the devotees, saints and poets of the Puṣṭi-Mārgi Ballav community were kirtankārs. In the Rām snehi community also the position of Saṇkirtan was very high. Kabir Das himself was famous as a Sankirtankār. In the Malbi folk-culture, as a medium of Bhakti cult Sankirtan is very popular, Even now in the temples of Malaba during religious festivals like Rām Janma, and Krishṇa Janma, sankirtan and recital of devotional songs are arranged by various Bhajan Maṇḍalis. In the region of Mahārāstra among various communities the Barkāri community is very prominent. This is a Saṇkirtan oriented community. The primary motto of this community are Hari Saṇkirtan and social service. It is believed that this community was started by Santh Gyāneśwar a great preacher of Bhakti movement. In this community, people of various Castes and creeds forgetting their individual difference exhilarate themselves in the Sankirtan of Bhagwān Biṭhalesh and travel in milions to Pandharpur, during the 11th day of the month of Kartika and Aṣhadha. It is a fine example of social and national Integration. Behind the back ground the religious aspirations of this community the principles of growth of the nation can be found. Maharastrian saints like Nām Dev Eknāth and Tukārām are prominent who endeavoured hard from the beginning to eradicate social discriminations and to achieve social equality by uniting the society irrespective of Caste and creed, through Kirtan Bhakti. The Abhangas of famous Barkari Saiṅt Behana Bai, who was a disciple of santh Tukaram are famous Maharastrian kirtan songs.

The impact of Nām Saṇkirtan and Bhagan is seen in entire south India. In the growth and flow of Bhakti tradition in India the 'Alwar' devotees of Tamil Nadu occupy a prominent position. The Saṇkirtan granta of this community is named as "Dibya Prabandhaṁ". It contains collection of four thousand hymns. The Alwars regard it as the Veda of Tamil language. The Folk institution kirtan was used as a medium to spread Bhaktirasa among the people in the entire region of Braj, Rajas-than and Malab by the lady singer "Chandra Sakhi" through her simple and sweet folk songs. All the Bhakti poets and saints of Gujarat like Santh Mahi Das, Santh Lal Bapu, Santh Bhimsaheb, Santh Hothiji, Santh Dasijivanji Santh Narsim Mehta, were kirtan lovers, and kirtan was their medium of propagation. From among them Bhaktidhāra of kirtan lover devotee Narsim Meheta provided inspiration to the father of the Nation Mahatma Gandhi during the national freedom movement. The kirtan song of this poet "Baishnab Janato..."was the most favourite Bhajan of Mahatma Gandhi. Even the word 'Harijan' was also found by Mahatma Gandhi from the kirtan song of devotee Narsim Meheta learning from the Gujarati Kirtan institution and Bhakti Dhārā about 'Ahimsā' or Non-Violence, Mahatma Gandhi was able to unite India and propagate the ideals of universal brotherhood. In the saint like conduct of Mahatma Gandhi the influence of Gujarati Bhakti movement is notable.

In the 12th century A. D., in the religious history of entire Eastern India an extra-ordinary novelty was brought in by Bhakta Kabi Sri Jayadev of village Kenduli in Puri District of Orissa State. The Iśuddha Bhaktibād of Śrī Chantanya Dev owes its origin to the "Gīta Govinda" of Śrī Jayadev. In the field of Bhakti literature for the first time the character of Rādhā was beautifully presented in "Gīta Govinda" Even in Rajasthani literature and in the Radha Krishna eternal love poems of Mirābāi the influence of "Gīta Govinda" is very significant. Among the four most famous kirtankārs, poets and saints of Eastern India notably Sri Jayadev, Sri Chaitanya Sankar and Bidyāpati, the Oriya poet Sri Jayadev was the pioneer. His influence on others is crystal clear. In the whole of India after the Alwar community only Srī Jayadev started composing songs and Saṇkirtans about the Rādhā-Kṛiṣhṇa eternal love. Now also in various parts of India has composition 'Gīta Govinda' is sung by innumerable Saṇkirtan groups. To propagate his Bhakti cult Srī Chaitanyadev emphasized on the role of Saṇkirtan so greatly that it is not possible to separate the word Saṇkirtan from the Chaitanya and especially becanse of Sri Chaitanya Bengal is known as the land of 'Kirtan' Sri Chaitanya Dev propagated Saṇkirtan in the state of Bengal and Orissa. The "Gīta Govinda" of Srī Jayadev was very dear to Sri Chaitanya. Among the various kirtan epics of Bengal 'Billwamaṇgal's 'Krishna Karnāmruta' and innumerable kirtan poems of Chaṇḍī Das and Bidyāpati are notable. At a later phase, Bidyāpati resided in Mithila and was known as the 'Maithili Kokila.' Maithila was one of the 'Panch Goudas'. The propagater of Bhakti cult, Som Mishra was a Maithili poet. The birth place of Srī Chaitanya Dev 'Nadia' was also totally influenced by the Saṇkirtans. Even now among the various forms of Saṇkirtan one Nandiā-Kirtan type of Saṇkirtan is prevalent. The names of many Bengali Bhakti poets like Rupa Goswāmī, Jiva Goswāmī, Murārī, Lochan Dās, Brundāban Das Jayananda, Govind Das, Chānd Kāji, poet Ullauddin Murtaja Ali, find special mention in the field of Krishna Lilā and Chaitanya Lilā. The 'Saptakaṇḍī Rāmāyan' written in Payār Chanda' by Bhakta Kabi Śrī Krutibāsa is beautiful poem about Rām Saṇkirtan and it is extremely popular in the whole of Bengal like "Tulsi Rāmāyan".

During the Bhakti period Assamese saint poet Sankar Dev travelled the whole of India and propagated the message of unity. Selecting and incorporating from the various languages of India. Śankar Dev enriched the Assamese language. This saint was a great propagator of Baiṣhṇabite Bhakti cult. In the history of Assamese Literature the period 1449 A. D. to 1650 A.D. is called the Baiṣhṇab period because of the influence of Sankar Dev's writings. The Bhakti path of Sankar Dev is known as 'Ekśaran' and this was propagated by him through Kirtan literature and Saṇkirtan. 'Kirtan Ghoṣā' is a very prominent composition of this poet.

There are two faces of the folk institution Sankirtan notably-Samyak and Samabetik. Samabetik kirtan is mainly known as Kirtan. Its position is very high in the society. This was a justified medium of Bhakti movement as it was able to unite all irrespective of Caste, Creed and religion and the great saints, philosophers and devotees were able to creat universal brotherhood and friendship through it. 'Baul' community of Bengal originated bearing the influence of Hindu Bhakti cult and suffism from the back ground of folk institution Sankirtan which is the greatest folk institution of the Bhakti movement period. So the role of Sankirtan is no loss in maintaining national unity.

TYPFS OF BHAKTI BASED FOLK INSTITUTIONS IN INDIA :

ASSAM

In Assam there are plenty of devotional folk institutions and folk songs among which Deul festival of Barpeta is most remarkable. Barpeta in northern Kamrup district of Assam was a great centre of Bhakti movement and "Baishnaism". Deul or Doul Yāṭrā is purely religious based on Baishnabite Bhakti thought and synchronises with Holi. The 'Satra' or monastery was founded by Śrī Mādhāva Deva, the Principal disciple of Śrīśankardev. His influence over the Barpetans is very deep. The kīrtan Ghar is the main shrine where all regular Baishnaba religious functions are held daily on the second day of the Doul Yatra besides the regular religious rituals, drummers and musicians perform a Bhaona, a traditional Baishnab Theatrical performancc. The Deity of this festival is Mahāprabhu Kāliā Ṭhākur (Śrī Kṛiṣhṇa) and there are many similarities with the Car festival of Lord Jagannāth of Puri.

Folk songs like Nāāms and Geets are the real reflection of Baishnab influence, in Assamese folk literature. The term 'Naam' signifies the name of God and is also widely used to mean the devotional folk songs of Assam, for example Gosain Naam, deal with the story of the Lilā of Śrīkṛiṣhṇa. Vrindāban Nāām deal with the Lila of Śrīkṛiṣhṇa at Vrindaban.

The Deh Bikarar Geet of Assamese esoteric sects (known as Ratikhowā, Ritiyā, Purnasevā, Gopidharā etc) are enriched with spiritualism and Bhakti philosophy. Scholars consider the style of this songs as similar to Vaishnaba songs and many of them also glorify the name of Madhava Deva, the famous Vaishnava preacher-poet.

Sikirs & Jaris are devotional songs of Assamese Muslims, Zikirs have been describes as the 'Islamic Counter part of 'Deh

Bikarar Geet' The Khol, mṛidaṇga and cymbals are the principal folk musical instruments of vaishnab folk songs and dances in Assam.

RAJASTHAN :

In Rajasthan, Bhajans and Banis are devotional folk songs which are very popular among the Harijans, Chamārs, Bhaṇghis, Balais and Rahgars. By these songs India's spiritual heritage and philosophical tradition of Bhakti are carried to the humblest strata of the society. Bhajans and Banis are sung to the accompaniment of the Folk musical instruments like Ektārā, Ḍholak, Gini, etc. in night long sat-sangs. The Bhajans composed by Mirābāi, a great female saint of Bhakti movement, and a great devotee of Śrīkṛishṇa are sung with special devotion in Rajasthani folk lore.

PUNJAB :

Most of the Punjabi folk songs. dances and festivals have its devotional value. Punjab is the land of the Vedas, and the land enriched by the experiences of saints and sages. So the Punjabi folk songs are abounding in the eulogies of famous gurus, bhagats and yogis like Guru Nānak Dev, Guru Govind Singh, Farid, Nām Dev, Gopi chand, Bhartruhari and Puran who have played pivotal roles in the propagation of Bhakti movement. There are devotional folk songs about Indra, Brahma, Saraswati, Vaiṣhno Devī, Ramachandra and Seetā and many others narrate about Kṛiṣhṇacharita to create Bhakti emotion in the heart of the people. The Guruparabs and other festivals of Punjab are purely devotional in character Some festivals are held in Punjab in honour of the Śikh gurus who were the real guide of humanity and also the country. The Sikh gurus were highly religious and patriotic to the bone. In Guruparabs Guru Nānak Dev, Guru Govind Sing, and Guru Arjun Dev are revered and remembered by the people.

In this occasion in different places religious congregations are held and hymns from the "Grantha Sāheb" are chanted. Undoubtedly, Grantha Saheb is the reflection of Indian 'Bhakti-Tatwa' through the ages.

MADHYA PRADESH :

The folk musical materials of Madhya Pradesh may broadly be classified into three groups. The first in the tribal songs which are undoubtedly very rich in content. The second group is about the country side song. It includes legendary narratives, ceremonial songs, worksongs and the songs linked with rituals, love and different professions. The third group of folk songs have a close affinity with Bhakti cult of the mediavel period. The Vast concourse of these songs draw thems from mythology and ranges from the traditional Harikathā to the simple rendering of old Bhajans and Arti songs of Chandra Sakhi, Sukhai, and the devotional songs attributed to Rām Dev. Thousands of songs and Baiṣhṇabite padas are sung with immense religious favour.

CHHATISGARH

The different aspect of the folk literature of Chhatisgarh is inextricably linked with Bhakti thought. Taking into consideration the Bhaktirasa, Danda is primarily male oriented folk dance. Danda is being named as 'Rāsa' in the Chhatisgarh region. To perform this dance the male villagers came out in Baishnabi costume with 'Tilak' on their forehead and with garlands. Adorned with colourful attire each of them holds a 'Daṇḍa' or stick in his hand. They dance in a circular way, with a particular rhythem striking the stricks of each other and creating a specific music in a highly artistic manner. Viewing this dance one is reminded of the "Madhur Nrutya" of Lord Kṛiṣhna with the Gopa boys. Generally this dance continues from the day of Sukla ekadasi in the month of Kartika to

Phalgun Purnima. The songs of this dance are based on the Bhaktirasa of Rāmāyaṇ, Mahābhārata and Kṛiṣhṇa Kathā of Bhagabat.

The influence of Bhakti movement of medieval period is highly discernible in many devotional songs in the folk literature of Chatisgarh region. In these devotional songs different religious views and sects find revealation. The number of oral devotional songs are much more than the devotional songs in written form by different saints and prophets.

In the Bhajan literature of chhatisgarh region the impact of pioneering Nirgun Saints Santh Kabir, Jivan Dash, and Dharam Dash is highly conspicuous. In the back ground of these devotional songs a society free of caste. creed and colour finds its true devotional manifestation. These 'Bhajans' are balanced between Nirguṇ and Saguṇ trends. The 'Madaee' dance of Chhatisgarh region is also one kind of Bhakti dance. Another male oṛiented folk dance of Chhatisgarh region held in the month of Phalguna is also one type of 'Rāsa' The Chhatisgarh 'Pandāvani' can also be regarded as a medium of Bhakti movement considering its moral theme.

HARYANA :

The cherished value of devotion plays a very significant role in the life of Haryana folk community. The devotioṅ reflected in the folk songs is not the devotion of a particular caste or religion but of the whole community in Haryana. The devotional folk songs of this tract are classified into two sections.

1. Mangal Geet for the deities 2. Bhajans. These two sections of devotional folk songs are full of Bhakti thoughts.

Some folk songs belonging to the first section bring out the images of Baba Bhumian, Baba Hori Das, Sanjhi, Sayeedpir and Guga Pir etc. Particualarly Sayeedpir songs show the unity of Hindu and Muslims as the Hindus also worship Sayeed pir, a muslim Deity. Sayeed is considered to be the preceptor of both Hindu and Muslims.

At village Jharoda, near Bahadurgarh in Rohtak district, every year a fair is held twice in the memory of Baba Hari Das, a popular saint of Bhakti movement.

Bhajans are the purely devotional folk songs in praise and honour of Rāma, Kṛishṇa. Rādhā, Bishṇu, Śiva and other Hindu gods nd goddesses, Some Bhajans deal with Philosophical and metaphysical thoughts of life and death, "which are two important aspects of Bhakti cult. This thought leads the devotees to promote a pious and pure life.

FOLK—INSTITUTIONS OF ORISSA.

During the 14th century A. D. many Hindus of Northern India accepted Islam as their religious coming under the terror tactics aad various temptations. Many rules, rituals and conservatism entered into Hindu religion for fear of the muslim rulers. Paradāh system, untouchability and Barṇāśhrama dharma again got reinstated. In the other hand coming under the influence of Brāhminism the Hindu scriptures written in Sanskrit remained confined to the exclusive group of Brāhmin Pandits. The general people could not touch the theme, moral and wisdom of these scriptures. In this time, especially in the social life of entire Northern India anarchy continued because of the oppression of the muslims, Naturally Hindu—Muslim enemity grew, In course of time many Sadhus, Saints and preachers wanted to create a harmony in between the religions to save the country from religious conversion. Under these circumstances the Indian Sadhus, Saints and Poets tried their best to popularise Hindu religion. This period became the growing period for the literature and languages of Eastern and northern

India. To popularise the religion the sadus and saints used the mother tongue of the people while preaching from the scri tures and Holy books. Religion became simple easy and free from the practice of Barnāśhrama in place of the earlier complexities and puritanism of Brāhminism. This is Bhakti-dharma and this movement is Bhakti movement, During this period Nilāchal or Śrīkhetra of Puri became the centre of Bhaktidharma in the entire Eastern India where from very ancient time there was the light of Bhakti and brotherhood. For this reason starting from the 10th century to the 16th century all the Sadhus and saints, devotees, poets and preachers of India came to Puri or Nilāchal and Stayed here. Even today in Nilachal Dhām of Puri, the Maths of Santh Kabir Garib Das, Guru Nanak Dev, Tulsi Das, Gharan Das exist The Nilāchal puruṣhottam Khetra of Puri was the sacred place of the various religious cults of Norther, Eastern, and Southers India from the 11th or 12th century A. D.

There is no distinction between the ancient Oriya Bhakti literature and the Santh Literature of Northern India. in the ancient Oriya Bhakti literature and Sagun Nirgun Bhajans hundreds of Non-Oriya Baishnab compositions are found. In no other Indian literature this speciality is there. Many Bhajans of Santh Kabir, Nanak, Charan Das, Daria and Dadu are propagated through the folk institutions of Orissa. When the entire Northern India was terrified and politically unstable by the muslim invasions, Orissa was the only state in the whole of North and Eastern India where peace was there. This land was a fully independent Hindu state and its religion was a truly humanistic one based on the principles of Bhakti brotherhood parity and oneness. So, during the Bhakti movement period also, Orissa had nothing to learn about National Integration through the medium of Bhakti-cult. Especially, Orissa is the pioneer and teacher to the whole of India in this respect. The sacred land Orissa has retained this speciality till now. The role of different Folk institutions of Orissa in the propagation of Bhakti-cult may shortly be described as noted below.

Truly, Orissa can be regarded as the land of inspiration for the Bhaktimovement. The great flow of Bhakticult coming from different regions of India assembled in Puri of Orissa and Lord Jagannath has been transformed into the symbol of a National God. In the propagation of Bhakti movement in Orissa numerous saints collaborated actively with innumerable Folk Institutions of Orissa. In the prepared article some of the most prominent folk-institutions of Orissa are discussed briefly.

Oriya Saṇkirtan :

In Orissa, there has been a colourful tradition of Saṇkirtan which is a folk institution of Bhakti cult. Already a tradition to propagate the eternal love story of Rādhā and Kṛishna through the medium of Kirtan was created from the time of Oriya poet Śrī Jayadev, the composer of 'Gīta Govinda' much earlier than the Kirtan institutions of the Assamese Poet Śankar Dev and Mahātmā Śrī Chaitanya Dev. From that period onwards Oriyā saṇkiran is being propagated through different styles. As a whole the kirtans in vogue in different regions of Orissa can be classified into three categories.

(1) Bhajan Saṇkirtan : Nadiā Kirtan, and the Rangiā Kirtan of Western Orissa based on the themes of the Ranga Abatar of Srikrishna.

(2) Nām Sankirtan : It is the result of the Goudiya Baishnab Sampradāya and the Utkaliā Baishnab Sampradāya. Both the Sampradāyas engage in propagating their respective sampradaya's "Tāraka Brahmanaāma" through the medium of Saṇkirtan.

(3) Nāām Jagyan Saṇkirtan : The other name of this is "Prahari" This folk institution is based on the "Chatuhṣaṣṭhī Dandātmikā Lilā" of Baiṣhṇab theme. This Nāām Jagyan Saṇkirtan is named according to its duration as Aṣṭa Praharī, 24 Praharī, and 108 Praharī etc. specially it is held during the time of Kartika Purnima and Palguna Purnima. Under the incentive of one village and with the co-operation of neighbouring villages it is organised. The Pujā Mandap of Nāam Jagyan Sankirtan is devided into two parts such as.

(a) Jagyan Mandap or Rāhāsa Kunja and
(b) Rāhāsa Mandali.

The "Tāraka Brahmanāāma" is recited in the Jagyan Mandap and different Saṇkirtan groups dance and recite the 'Nāām' in the circular Rāhāsa Mandalī. The various musical instruments used in Saṇkirtan and Mṛidaṇga, Mardala, Karatāla, Jhānja, etc. Nāām Jagyan Sankirtan is especially prevalent in the Western Orissa.

'Pālā' :

In Orissan folk-culture during the 'Nāām giving ritual of the newly born cheld Satya Nārāyan Pujā is held. Religiously 'Pālā' is attached to this ritual. In India to bring in Hindu-Muslim cultural harmony many endeavours have been attempted and the Orissan folk-institution Pālā is one of them. It is a sweet amalgamation of Hindu-Bhakti cult and Muslim suffism. In Pālā Satyapīr is worshipped which is an ammalgamation of Hindu—Satyanārāyan and Muslim Pīr. Pālā is originated from the back ground of Bhakti movement for the eradication of the Hindu-Muslim enemity. Traditional Pālā is divided in the sixteen parts. So it is called as Solha-Pālā. The first pala is the Janma Pālā. In this, the subject of the creation of Pālā is described. The poet of Pālā literature is Kabi

Karṇapura. The role of Pālā as a medium of propagation for Bhakti movement can be described briefly.

During the middle age Indian empire in Various parts were captured by the Muslims and after that Hindu-Muslim conflicts continued in this country. The Muslims started oppressing Orissan Language, Literature and religion after conquering Orissa in the 16th century A. D. Aourangajeb had decreed to destroy all the newly built temples and not to sanction funds for the repair of old temples. The Muslims created terror in the heart of the Oriya people by attacking the Jagannāth temple repeatedly. As the last resort, according to history, a desperate king Ramachandra II embraced Islam and married a Muslim Girl only to save Jagannāth temple of Puri.

Gradually, in different places of Orissa Muslim localities and Masjids were setup. Among them the Cuttack Dewan Bazar Masjid (1685) Balu Bazar Juma Masjid (1690) Mahammadia Bazar Masjid and Kadam Rasul (1713) Jajpursahi Masjid (1686) are famous. Especially due to the oppressive tendency of some Muslims deep hatred and disbelief were created in the heart of the Oriyas and also Indians against the Islam religion. So, to create brotherhood, love and friendship in between both the communities of the society Kabir (1440-1510) Guru Nānak Dev (1469 to 1538) Dadu of Rajputana (1544 to 1603) and Prabhu Śyāmānanda and Rasikānand of Orissa worked tirelessly and created the New Bhakti movement.

Professing and propagating Bhakti movement Kabir N-ānak, Dadu and many other Indian saints came to Puri of Orissa and in Puri their 'Maths' still exist. Prabhu Rasika—Nanda could manage to transform the heart of the tyrant subedar Mohammad Beg by accepting him as his disciple and it instilled new hope in the heart of the Oriya people. Prabhu Śyāmānand accepted Bha kta Sālabeg as his disciple and it gave rise to a strong friendship between both the communities in Orissa. By observing the multifaced similarities in between the Koran of prophet Mahammad and Hinduveda and Puranas especially the closeness between the Islamic Panch Mela, Kalama, Namaj, Reja, Haf and Hindu 'Trisandhyā' saints like Kabir, Nānak, Dadu and Sri Chaitanya Dev tried to bring a harmony in between the Hindu and Islam religions from their point of views. Kabir had said Rām-Rahim and Krishna-Karim are just same God. Dadu had said Hindus and Muslims are like the two hands of God. In both the hands, when palms are not together, one can not drink the Amṛit. In all the time seciety is controlled by the sacred and idealistic thoughts of Mahāpurushas. The Oriya Hindu and Muslim society also came under the impact of 'Amṛitbāṇī' and the society under-went a great metamorphosis. Gradually point of views changed, every one considered each other as brothers and as an integral part of the society, by giving up intolerance towards each others religions. Hindus and Muslims started showing respect to each others Gods and Religions. Pālā originated in this harmonious back ground as the sacred symbol to this sweet union. There remained no distinction between Rām-Rahim, Kṛiṣhṇa-Karim, Jagannāth Kohda, Pir-Satyanarayan, Koran and the Purāṇs. The Prasad of Satyapir 'Sirini' became acceptable in all homes. That is why in Janma Pālā Satyapīr has clearly said that—

"Jagannāth Rupī Āmi Oḍiṣhāte Āra
Hindu Muslamān Sarba Kari ekākāra"

To describe the Lilā of Satyapīr in Pālā mentioning his close affinity with different Abatāārs in Hindu purāṇa is very significant in the context. Harmony is achieved in Pālā between the Oriya, Bengali and Parsee languages. Bhakta Kabi Bharat chandra (1707-60) the composer of 'Annada Maṅgala' and Satya-Pīr-Pāñchālī in Bengali literature travelled various places of Orissa from 1742-45 and stayed for sometime in the Kabir

Maṭh in Puri. In the Bengali society "Satyapīr-Pānchālī" is read during the religious ceremony of Satya Nārāyan Pujā. Likewise in Oriya Society at the time of Satyanārāyan Pujā the glory of Satyapīr is presented which is known as Pālā. During the sojourn of Bharat chandra in Kabir Math, Poet Kar-ṇpura composed the Pālā coming under his influence.

So, it can be accepted that Pālā originated in the year 1742. Kabir's religious ideology and Bhakti consciousness get reflected to a great extent in Pālā-Kabir has granted equal status to Ram-Rahim and Koran-Puran. In Pālā it is also said--

"Rām mahim Jana Korān Purāne"

The ways of Pujā as delineated by the Karṇapura in Pālā also presents religious harmony.

In the Folk culture of Orissa the pujā of Satyapīr and Pālā are truely mirrors of the Harmonious Bhaktibād. Till the present day in the Puja of Satyapīr both Brāhmin and Muslim priests including Āchaṇḍāla Ājabana Participate with great devotion. At present Pālā is a popular folk institution responsible for the popularisation of Ancient Oriya literature. In the connection the Burro-Nat or Burro Kathā of South India is a similar folk institution like Pālā.

Dāskāṭhiā

Dāskāṭhiā, which owes its origin from Dās Bhakti thought, was once upon a time a most popular Folk-Institution of Ganjam district only. But later on it spread to other parts of Orissa. In Bhakti sense 'Dāsa' means a pure devotee and Kāthi means-two wooden pieces played in tune with the devotional songs of the devotees. Two of the most eminent personalities of Dās Bhakti known to us from Religious scriptures are Bishnu Kirtankār Nārad and Rām Kirtankār Hanumān. Both these Biṣṇu devotees were always found with devotional songs on their lips and Dāskāthi in their hands. Perhaps the folk institution Dās Kāthiā finds its origin from this tradition.

It means that any one who plays and sings devotional songs by means of 'Dāskəthi' is known as 'Dāskāthiā' Only two persons participate in 'Dāskāthiā' One is the 'Gāyaka' (Chief singer) and the other is known as the 'Pāliā' who helps the Gāyaka in all respects of singing, dancing, and action. They present the religious and devotional 'Charitas' from Rāmāyaṇ, Mahābhārata, Kṛiṣhṇakatā, Śiva Purāṇa and other Aṣṭādasha purāṇas. At present it is also a popular media for papularisation of ancient oriya literature.

Daṇḍanāṭa :

Daṇḍanāta is performed through the Fair-medium of 'Daṇḍa Yātrā' in Orissa. Daṇḍa Nāta can be accepted as folk religious institutions of the Tandave Rudra worship. The time bound impact of Śaiba, Matta Mayura Śaiba, Tantra, Sākta, Gānapatya and Baiṣhṇabite religion are clearly visible in Daṇḍa Nāta. The traditional Daṇḍa consists of sixteen Suānga. In the background of Baiṣhṇaba nrutya, yoginī nrutya, Ḍāhikhelā nrutya Bāidhana nrutya, Biṇā Kāliyā nrutya, the glory of Bhakti cult is propagated. From a very early time how Daṇḍanāta was propagating the message of Bhakti cult in the society, the following examples justify it ably :

(1) In this Nāta everyone participates starting from the Brāhmins to the Chaṇḍālas.

(2) The Mālis and Brāhmins together worship Dakhin Kālī and Kalā Rudramaṇi Śiva—The main deity of Daṇḍa.

(3) About the origin of Daṇḍa, the Bhaktas or Danduās tell a myth which is about meditation or the Tapasyā

of Sudraka of the Rāmāyan period which generate popular opinion about the eradication of the practice of 'Barna' system in the society.

(4) Bhakti, as the finest path for the Gruhasthi is being propagated through the medium of 'Yogi Nrutya' in Danda.

The Kośalī Daṇḍa seen in the Western Orissa which is also known as 'Keli' and 'Rangiā Danda' is wholly based on the theme of Kṛiṣhṇa Bhakti and Baishnabite cult. It is named as 'Keli' or 'Rangiā Danda' as the Lilā of Kṛiṣhṇa is the Chief subject of this Daṇḍa Nāṭa.

Folklore of Banjārās :

Some of the Banjārā folk-songs and folk dances are rich with religious and devotional value in Orissa. Being a nomadic and wide spread tribe, Banjārā in folklore have a remarkable similarity in their mode. The Banjārās of Rajasthan, Gujarat, Mahārāṣṭra, Madhya Pradesh, Western Orissa and South-eastern part of the country belong to same group. The Banjārās of Western Orissa known as 'Laban' are originally 'Lamana' Banjara migrated from Mahārāstra. They worship to Guru Nānak Dev, Kabir Dās, Sur Dās and Mirā Bāi. Most of the folk-songs used by 'Labanas' are composed by Kabir Das, the prominent prophet of Bhakti movement. The followings are some folk-items of Labanas relating with Bhakti cult.

(1) Festivals—Like Nānak Jayanti, Holi, Diwali etc.
(2) Kruṣhṇa Lilā.
(3) Nirguṇ-Bhajans.
(4) Dohā.
(5) Roji Baiṭhakī-Bhajani.
(6) Rām Bhajana or Pārāyan.

The Labana use Ḍholak, sticks, Khanjar, big sized earthern pot and Gini as their folk-musical instrument.

Karmā

Currently, Karmā is a typical tribal religious festival or Pujā which owes its origin from the thought of "existance of Karma Swāmī" of Indian cultural tradition. Tribes like Binjhal, Munda, Oram, Gandā, Mirthā, Khadia, Saharā, Kulī, Bhumij, Jharā and Chamār consider this festival as their traditional rituals. There are various types of Karmā namely "Baḍkarmā, Sānkarmā, Laxmīkarmā, Kadokarmā Kālīkarmā, Jhulan Karmā, Rijhen Karmā, Chalit Karmā, a Kheḍ Karmā, Meri Karmā, Duhura Karmā, Bauli Karma, and Keli Kadam Karmā, etc. Among these Kelikadam Karma reflects the Radhakruṣhṇa Bhakti cult. The main Deities of this performance is also Rādhā and Śrīkruṣhṇa Similarly in Karma, some of the couplets of Ḍhāpgeet and Ghumurāgeet (Tribal folk-dance of Kandha tract) are seen and are enriched with Bhakti thoughts, especially with Nirguṇa Bhakti.

Folklore of Bairagis :

In the Western part of Orissa, there live a pure Baisnavites-Identified as Bairāgī caste. Though they are Bairāgīs they are not hermits and they live a house hold life and they depend on alm for their livelihood by propagating the 'Bhakti Dhārā, Though they are not Brahmins yet they use to carry sacred thread, 'Tilak' Rudrakshya and wear saffron attire. They generally use 'Das surname' which is a general surname of all Bairāgis, devotees, and Saints. They are divided into five sub-sects as Girī, Purī, Ban, Bhāratī and Kośalī. They have a very rich folk lore tradition, which is filled with both 'Saguṇa' and 'Nirguṇa' Bhakti principles. The folklore can be divided into five divisions. (1) Śuddha Bhakti Bhajan (2) Sarir Bheda Bhajan (3) Bhakti Gāthā, (4) Suāṅga

(5) Sampradā Nrutya. They present their Bhajans with the help of 'Khānjani' 'Ektārā (Gopibādya) and 'Sāraṇgī' like musical instruments. Some of them are composed by Achyutānanda Das, Santh Niranjan Das, Arakhita Dās, Hāḍipɐ Das, Virasing Dās, Yaśobanta Dās, Ananta Dās, Gorekha Dās, Lui Das, Gunduchī Dās, Sermeṇā Das, Ghusuri Dās, Bāidhara Das, Bāppahana Dās, Chandramaṇī Das, Chaitanya Dās, Mukunda Das, Bihāri Das etc, and most of them are folk songs. They sing Bhakti gāthās with the help of Sāraṇgī which are the religious life story of different devotees of India, 'Suāṇga' is a lyrical folk drama, Using this means, the Bairāgīs propagate the life story of different saints and devotees in a rural areas. The story of the 'Suāṇgas' are mainly derived from the holy scriptures like 'Rāmāyāṇa', Mahābhārata' 'Dā ḍhyatā Bhakti rasāmruta' and Haribanśa. The 'Darḍhyata Bhakti rasāmruta' is a valuable holy book with collections of sixty six biographies of eminent kings and Baisnavites of different races of Purana and Bhakti Age, in which divine life of different saints and devotees have been depicted. In this context of Life story of Raghuarakṣhita, Raghu Behera, Madhabāchārya, Jholiā Kabir, Maṇi Dās, Kruṣhṇa Das, Gaṇapati Bhatta. Ananta Sabara, Melachha Lālbeg O Sālbeg, Dāsiā Bāuri, Tulsī Dās, Siputi, Mangal Goud, Mochi Rāma Das, Pipā Das, Mirā Bāi, Anand Sabara, are highly significants. The moral themes of these suaṇgas are (1) To seek Caste is obstacle to salvation (2) Bhakti is the right path for a 'Gruhasti'.

The folkdance of Bairāgīs is known as 'Sampradā' It is male dominated and three persons take part in it. The singer himself plays the 'Mrudaṇga' and two fellow-reciters namely "palia" take part in the recital with their Jhānjhas. The central theme of this dance is the 'Kriṣhṇa Story' and 'Daśābatār Charita' The main singer is known as 'Bāhāka' 'Gāhāka' or 'Bhat'. The style of playing 'Mrudaṇga' is based on classical form and he plays it in different 'Tālas' and 'Mātrās' among which

'Rudratāla' Brahmatāl 'Niskarā' Aṣṭamangala 'Krushṇatāla' and Rāmtāla are important. The sampradā tradition led to the emergence of folkdance Sanchāras which is at present the popular, religious and general folkdance of Western Orissa based on 'Bhaktidhārā' Now a days, the female are also taking part in the Bhakti dance 'Sanchāra'.

Though some of the Bairāgis identify themselves as Puṣṭi Margīya Ballava Sampradāya and some of them classify themeselves as Rāmānand Sampradāya yet most of them identify their 'Sampradāya' and 'Gotra' as Achyuta' Sākhā-Ananta gotra and Devata—'Jagannatha' From this point of view they may be regarded as 'Pure Utkaliyā Vaishnaba Sampradāya'.

Krushna Guru Bhajan :

The most popular folk-institution of Kruṣhṇa Bhakti movement in the western part of Orissa is Kruṣhṇa Guru Bhajan Maṇḍalī or the Kruṣhṇa Guru Bhajan. Its beginning could be traced to the first decade of the 16th century, probably in the year 1510 A. D. The folk-institution as reflected in legend, was started by a Vishnu-devotee belonging to Teli Caste Sri Chaitanya Dev, while propagating śuddhabhakti-Vaiṣhṇaba-Dharma started from Bengal and reached at Puri through Western part of Orissa. The Saṇkirtan was the most popular medium of Śrī Chaitanya Dev, for the propagation of Bhakti, from this style of Sankirtan Folk-institution named as "Krishna, Guru Bhajan" originated in western part of Orissa, which is a perfect medium for the propagation of Bhakti movement. The Kruṣhṇa Guru Bhajan is classified into four categories, such as 'Baiṭhakī, Nagar Kirtan, Nrutya and Lilā. The folk songs which are used in the Kruṣhṇa Guru Bhajan carry themes from literature of epics like Bhāgabata, Mahābhārat, Kruṣhṇa Kathās and Haribanśa Purāna. The Vaiṣhṇavites divide Bhakti into nine types such as Bastly Bhakti, Sakhya Bhakti, Dasya Bhakti and prema Bhakti. etc. All these nine Bhaktis find its expression in the Krușhņa Guru Bhajan. Moreover, Bhakti is known to Lord Krușhņa as the only God of the Universes and who as the teacher for the salvation are known as Krușhņa Guru Bhajan. Even though in Krușhņa Guru Bhajan the Aieswarjya Lila is depicted, its main purpose is the Madhurya Bhakti.

Nirguna Bhakti and Khanjani Bhajan :

The Nirguna Bhakti cult is considered as the most reformative cult during the Bhakti movement period. Some general features of Nirguna Bhakti Dhārā are—

(1) The cult was started by the poets of the so called lower classes of people in the society.

(2) Their religious thought and feeling were simple, yet very vast.

(3) They have clarified the basic thought and the primary aims of Dharma, relegating into back ground the worthlessness of traditional saguna mode of worship.

(4) They had to throw into the wind-the superstitious, obscurantist and blind beliefs and professed in the society for a pure, simple and Dharma oriented trend of living.

(5) There was no place for casteism in the Nirguņa Bhakti Dhārā.

Kabir Das is regarded as the greatest saint poet of Nirguņa Jnānāshrayee Branch of Bhakti Age. Based on the theory of Nirguna Bhakti Dhārā and Adweytabād (Monism), a reform oriented new religious cult has risen in Orissa in the 19th century A. D. This Dharma which was started by Śrī Mukund Dās or Mahimā Gosāin called as Mahimā Dharma or Alekha Dharma. The best Chārana poet of this Dharma is the saint-poet Bhimā Bhoi. He was born in a 'Kaņḍh' scheduled caste family. All the treasures of Mahimā Dharma have been given life and propagated by the saint poet Bhimā Bhoi. In the Philosophy of literature of Kabir Dās and Bhimā Bhoi a lot of similarities are disernible. The Kumbhpaṭiās or the Mahimā Dharmīs are classified in to Parā, Aparā, Āśrita and Bairāgi catogories and they propagate the Mahimā Bhakti thought by singing the devotional songs and couplets of Bhimā Bhoi. Like the Kirtan institution of Śrī Chaitanya Dev, Bhimā Bhoi also propagated his Bhakti literature through the folk-institution of Khañjaṇi Bhajan. This type of folk-institution are prevalent even today. The Khañjani Bhajan is performed in Baiṭhakī by single person or in a chorus. This style of performance of propagating Nirguṇa literature by means of Khañjaṇī Bhajan is seen in the whole of central and Eastern India. The yogīs, Bairāgīs and saints in Orissa also propagate the ancient Nirguṇa Bhajan literature by means of Khañjani. The following messages are propagated in the society by the Kumbhpatiās by singing the couplets and songs of Bhima Bhoi with the help of 'Khañjani'.

(1) Let my life be in Hell
Let others be in Heaven.
(2) Let the Dharma be blamed.
but let the world live, and
let Earch, Sky and space always smile.
(3) Man and Women are the two castes (Jāti)
and there is no other caste in this world.
(4) Niskāma (selfless) Nirguṇa Bhakti is the best Bhakti.
(5) All the immorality, oppression as discrimination
based on untouchability in this world can be
anhiliated by the Mahimā Dharma only.

Folk Lore of Debagunlas :

The Debaguniās are Chārana by occupation and reciters (Bards) of the Laxmī culture. The Chārana generally do not recognise Casteism. The ideal message of reformation has been well reflected in the 'Laxmī Gāthā' and 'Laxmī Suāṇga' from among the prevalent folklores of the Debagunias. The style of rendition of 'Laxmī Gāthā' and Laxmī Suānga' are different but their theme is generally same. The Laxmī Suāṇga' which is performed by them in the village roads is a form of folk-drama. The reformative spirit of the story in the 'Laxmī Suāṇga' can be briefly narrated like this. "The Thursday is the day of worship of Goddess Laxmī the eternal wife of Lord Jagannāth. On this uspicious day she aecepts the worship from every one from Chaṇḍāla to Brāhmins. Once, when Goddess Laxmī was coming out of home of Śrīyā Chāṇḍāluṇī, she was spotted by Lord Balsram who was returning from hunting. In a very angry mood he immediately called for lord Jagannath and informed him, "Look, your wife has all along been mingling with the untouchables like the panas and chandals, and destroying the sanctity of the Śrī Mandir. So you must have either divorce her at once or else stay with your wife in the locality of the Chandāls, "he commanded Lord Jagannāth. As a result of this Chandaluni episode Lord Jagannath had to divorce Laxmi upon the command of brother Balaram. Laxmi while departing told Lord Jagannāth that he was father of the Universe, but it was so strange that he was discriminating among his own sons on the grounds of Caste and race. "O.K. I am leaving, she told Lord Jagannāth but remember, you both brothers won't get any food, so long as you do'nt take food from this chāṇḍāluṇi, that is myself "Laxmī is the Goddess of Wealth. After her departure the Śrīmandir lost all its opulence, glaze and glory, and devoid of food and wealth. After a long painful period of turbulence, in a very dramatic manner they were forced to take food, prepared by Goddess Laxmi herself. Both of them begged for sincere appology and earnestly pleaded for her return to Śrī Mandir. She agreed upon the condition that henceforth there would not any place for caste feeling in the context of Bhakta and Bhakti and there would be no discrimination among people from Brahmins to Chandala in the Śrī Mandir and all would be treated alike. This fact was graciously accepted by Lord Jagannāth and Balavadra, Laxmī and Jagannāth were reunited.

Behind the background of this folklore, a strong reaction against Brāhminism finds expression in the depiction of character of the Goddess Laxmī. By transcending the barrier based on discrimination of untouchables, the glory of pure Bhakti Cult find its real imagination and true utterance. The spirit of reform which is revealed in this folklore preceeds the Bhakti movement of the middle age. Its influence is also highly discernible in the Oriya Maha Laxmī Purāṇa written by the said-poet Sri Balarām Das during the 16th century A. D.

Another form of folklore prevalent among the Debagunias is known as 'Śiśugītā' while begging for alm from door to door they sung this folk song with the help of 'Sārangi'. This folk song is based on the Bhakti theory and mixed with mysticism. Behind the background of this song the omnipresent eternal Brahma is depicted as a child. Like a mischivious and frivoious child the Creator of the Universe, is engaged in the task of creation and destruction, sitting of the path of eternity and timelessness. This peculier imagination of the Indian wisḍom find its expression in the 'Śisugītā' The Bālya Lilā as described in the literature of the most eminent saintpoet of Western Orissa Śrī Bhimā Bhoi, is also based upon this philosophical thought. Bhimā Bhoi has written in a devotional Song 'Bālaka parāye hoi, Abanā Mandire Thāin ; which means the Param Brahma remains in "Abanā Mandir" with the attitude of a child". The Bairāgī Sampradāya also propagates the 'Śiśugītā' with the help of Sārangi and the devotional songs of Bhimā Bhoi with 'Khañjani'.

Brata Katha :

Great affinity is there in between the existing "Bratas" of

Orissa and the flow of Bhakti cult. From very ancient time in Orissa many 'Bratas' and Oshas' are continuing. For ages together the story of 'Brata' and Osha' have enliven the Bhakti consciousness of the Society through the medium of folk culture/folk lore, and folk literature. From among them Sudaśhā Brata, Ruṣhi Pañchami brata, Nāpal Chauthi brata, Kedār Brata, Rabi nārāyaṇ Brata, Satyanārāyan Brata, Anantabrata, Rāi Dāmodara brata, Sombār brata, and Khudurukuṇī Oshā, Budhei oshā, Dutiyā Oshā, Alaṇā, Oshā, Baḍa Oshā, Bāli trutiyā Oshā, Dāluṇkā Oshā, Bhāi Jientiā Oshā, Dwitibāhan Oshā, etc, have become famous, Especially, to arrouse the sense of unity, dedication and devotion in the heart of women these 'Bratas' and Oshas, have originated. Some bratas have begotton for both brahmins and the non-brahmin caste. The ideals of equal and united society irrespective of caste and creed are revealed as the theme behind these Bratas and Oshas. Some bratas and oshas are Śākta, śaiba, Gāṇapatya, Baiṣhṇab and some have originated in different regions of the country. But generally all these types are inspired by the Bhakti consciousness of the Baishnabas and so are liberal in views. Especially based on Krishna Bhakti, Rai Damodar Brata and Kartika-Masanta is observed. The continuous flow of Bhajan, Kritan and Nāām Saṇkirtan based on Bhakti-thought are being observed through every villages of Orissa during the Kartika month.

Māhātmya :

Mahatmya is one of the many Bhakti based religious folk-institution in Orissa. Ekādaśī Māhātmya consists of 24 Ekadasis. Many occassional folk-institutions like Māgha Māhātmya, Baishākha Māhātmya, and Kartika Māhātmya are also seen in Orissa. During this time the Māhātmya literature composed by saint poets are read with deep devotion.

Melās

Melā described here is not like Sivaratri Melā, Kumbha melā or Makara melā. 'Melā' is one type of Bhakti institution like Brata and Oshā. In Orissa Trināth Melā, Panchānan Melā, Śani Melā, Bhāgabat Melā, are famous. By worshipping ones God and by reading the Melā-literature with devotion melā is observed. Many Sādhus and Saints have composed various melā literature. Generally these are composed in the Nabākhyarī style. At the starting of the mela the priest worships the deity of the Melā and then recites the religious Melā-geet. All the villagers irrespective of their caste, creed and colour listen to the Gēēt. Village singer groups are also present during the Melā and the singer groups recite the heart touching couplets in various 'Rāgas' and 'Rāgiṇīs' During this time folkmusic instruments like Mṛidaṇga, Mardala Gini, flute and Ghudukā etc. are used. Five to six types of recital styles are followed by the village singer groups for every couplet. Melā is declared over after completing the reading the Melā literature. Many morals are there in Melā literature like—

(1) All Humans are one.
(2) Service to the oppressed and poor is service to God.
(3) Casteism finds no place in Bhakti cult.
(4) One can attain God by pure devotion only.

'Bhāgabata Melā' :

Bhāgabata Melā is regarded as the greatest and most popular folk-institution of Baiṣhṇabite Bhakti-Movement in Orissa. In this institution the 'Oriya Bhagabata' written by Śrī Jagannāth Dās is worshipped and recited in Kirtan style inside the 'Gadi'. Sri Jagannāth Das belonging to the 16th century is the contemporary of Sri Chaitanya Dev. The role of his Oriya 'Bhāgabata' is very significant in the propagation of Bhakti movement and in the growth of Oriya language and literature.

'Bhāgabata Ṭuṇgī' or Bhāgabat Ghar' were established in very village of Orissa coming under the influence of his Oriyā Bhāgabata. These were truly the temples for special unity irrespective of Caste, Creed and high and low feelings. The Bhagabata Mela was much more influential in Orissa than the 'Kirtan' of Sri Chaitanya Dev. All the Oriyas consider the reading of 'Bhāgabata' as most essential in life like the 'Gītā' The Bhāgabata is like the religious and cultural constitution and the true guide of life for every Oriya. In Orissa, Folk institution like 'X Melās' originated coming under the impact of Bhakti-Grantha 'Bhāgabata'.

The human heart-string is thrilled most by music, and the transformation of human instinct is achieved through musical notes. Devotion is the sensitive, stable yet conviction of the innermost part of human heart. Because of this inter-relation it is easier to make the man reformative through devotional music by making him immersed in the ocean of Bhakti. All the literatures of Bhakti period are lyrical and poetical by nature. The Bhakti movement becomes successful with the help of literatures and connotations through these folk-institutions. So, these, folk-institutions play a great role in the propagation and spreading of Bhakti cult.

REFERENCES

1. Astadasha puranas with Sanskrit text.
2. Narada pancharatnam (Sanskrit)
3. Narada Bhakti Sutram („)
4. Mahabharatam („)
5. Valmiki Ramayanam („)
6. Ramanuja charya ka Vishistadeitika Bhakti darshan (Hindi)—Dr. Sarnamsing Arun.
7. Hindi Sahitya ka vrihat Itihas—Dr. Bhagavat sharan Upadhyaya.
8. Sri Sankara Charya—Pandit Valadev Upadhyaya.
9. Vagvat Sampradaya—Pandit Valadev Upadhyaya.
10. Hindutva—Ramdas Goud.
11. Sanskrit Sahitya Ka Itihas—Vachaspati Gaerola.
12. Uttaree Bharat ki Santh parampara—Parsuram Chaturvedi.
13. Suffeemat aren Hindi Sahitya—Dr. B. K. Jain.
14. Kerala ki bhakti Sadhana –Dr. M. Geoge.
15. Bhakti andolana Aur Islamee tatva chintanki mulbhul ekata—Dr. Ramprasad Tripathy.
16. Marathi Bhakti Sahitya—Prof. M. G. Deshpande.
17. Gujrati Sahitya ka Itihas—Sri Jayantakrishna Harikrushna Dev.
18. Bharateeya Darshan—Dr Umesh Mishra.
19. Telugu Sahitya ka itihas—Valsouri Reddy.
20. Alwar Bhaktonka Tamil Prabandham Aur Hindi Krishna kavya—Dr. Malik Mohammud.
21. Bhakti ka Vikarh—Dr. Munshiram Sharma.
22. Kavir Sahitya ka Adhyayana—Purusottamlal Sreevastava.
23. Kalyan (Sankirtana ka).
24. Vaisnavism, Saivism, and Minor Religious systems—R. C. Bhandarkar.
25. The Religion of Islam—Ali Moulana Mohammed.
26. Aspects of Early Vaisnavism—J. Gour.
27. Religion and philosophy of Rigveda and Upanisads-Keith.
28. The Origin and Development of Religion—S. B. Gould.
29. Religion in Vedic literature—S. P. Deshmukh.
30. Hindu castes and sects—T. Bhattacharya.
31. The Chaitanya Movement—T. Kennedy.
32. Village goes of South India—Witch head.
33. Folklore of Rajasthan—D. R. Ahuja.
34. Folklore of Madhya Pradesh—Shyam Parmer.

35. Folklore of Tamil Nadu—S. M. L. Lakshman Chettiar.
36. Folklore of Assam Jogesh Das.
37. Folklore of Punjab—S. Singh Bedi.
38. Folklore of Orissa—K. B. Das and IK Mahapatra.
39. Odia Sahityara Itihasa (Oriya)—Dr. Banshidar Mohanty.
40. Shreehari Sankirtana (Oriya)—Ed. Dr. Fakir Mohan Das.
41. Sohalapala (Oriya)—Kavi Karna pura.
42. Dardhyata Bhakti—Rasamrita (Oriya) Bhakta kavi Ram Das.
43. And the sources collected from field study by the author.

MATTAMAYURA SAIVISM IN ORISSA

4

MATTAMAYURA SAIVISM IN ORISSA

Dr. Ramprasad Mishra
Reader in History

Divergences in view, vow and Vistas generally schismatise a school of religion into a number of sub-sects. Śaivism, generally recognised as a primordial religious system from the standpoint of the phallic adoration was divided into a set of subsects because of these analogous variance in vows, views and vistas. While writing a pedantic commentary on Saḍdarśhanasamuccaya of Jain monk Haribhadra paudit Guṇaratna categorises the followers of Śaivism as (i) Śaivas (ii) Pāśupatas (iii) Mahābratadharas and (iv) Kālamukhas.[1] Ānandagiri in his work 'Śhaṇkaravijaya' classifies the schools of Śaivism as (i) Śaivas (ii) Roudras (iii) Ugras (iv) Jaṇgamas (v) Bhaṭṭas and (vi) Pāśupatas[2]. Mādhavāchārya in his Sarvadarśhanasamgraha divides the Śaiva followers as (i) Śaivas (ii) Nakuliśa pāśupata (iii) Raseśvara and (iv) Pratyabhijñā[3]. In many of the older Śaivite texts which record the categorisation of the followers of Śaivism a regular reference to the particular Śaiva sect is invariably traced out. This invariable reference amply proves that the Śaiva sect within the fold of Śaivism was a school of remote antiquity. According to Mādhavāchārya the pristine religious concept of this Śaiva sect was based on the Siddhānta doctrines of ancient Śaivāgamas.[4] As the Scholars of Śaivism believe in consonance with the narration of Śhaṇkarabhāṣhya grounded on Brahmasūtra and other Śaivite texts.[5] The Siddhanta doctrine in its primal concept was first propounded and propagated by Maheśvara. As it is believed, it was preached in so called divine language Sanskrit.[6] The iron curtain of obscurity has not yet been uplifted by the research scholars of Śaivism with regard to the identity of the Sanskrit Siddhāntatattva or Śaivāgamas composed bn Maheśvara. On the otherhand the ancient Śaivite text Śivadharmottara suggests, that these Siddhānta doctrines were composed and preached by the ascetics and āchāryas of Śaivism among their disciples in Sanskrit, prakrit and regional languages.[7] As the doctrine of Siddhānta was preached in Sanskrit, prakrit and regional languages and was accompanied with the immanent and transcendent concept of Lord Śiva, it is plausible to believe that it was evolved with the influence of both Drāviḍian and Āryan cultures.

Śaivāchārya Śrīkaṇṭha accepts Śveta as the primal exponent of Śaiva School.[8] In consonance with his view Śveta taught to the followers of Śaivism the doctrines of Siddhānta Śaivāgamas at first.[9] The vāyavīya Saṁhitā of Śivapurāṇa describes that Śiva appeared in the embodiment of Śveta before prajāpati Brahmā and instructed him on Śaivabrahmajñāna to reveal the magninimity of Śiva as the omnipresent, omniscient and omnipotent Brahman.[10] In this Samhitā of Śiva purāṇa, prakṛiti is depicted as Māyā and Maheśvara, as Māyīn, the master of Māyā.[11] Description in exact consimilitude is also found in Śvetāśvatara upaniṣad.[12] In view of the paucity of authentic evidences it is however difficult to particularise in a gun poin the exact time of the composition of this upaniṣada and to form a conclusive identity of its author. The nomenclature of this Upaniṣada as also the visible Śaivite influence on its theme however make us believe that doctrine of Śveta had more or less spread its shadow on the contents of this text. Among the earlier upaniṣadas of Indian culture this Upaniṣad is generally believed by the scholars to have registered a prominent place in its favour. Śvetāśvatara also figures as the first reverable ascetic among the leading Twenty-eight yogāchāryas of Vāyavīya Samhitā[13] who played remarkable role for the development of Śaivite yoga. Sometimes a misconception crawls into the impression of the scholars that the doctrines of Śaivāgamasiddhāntas are heterodox and antivedic in nature as they are not quoted in Śhaṇkarabhāṣya and Bhāsvatī commentary of paundit Bāchaṣpati Mishra and as they are described as anti-upaniṣhadic in few śaivite texts.[14] It is a gross mistake to subscribe congruence to this misconception because in Śvetāśvatara Upaniṣad and Vāyavīya Samhitā, prakṛiti is depicted as Māyā and Lord Maheśvara is described as Māyīn in a perfect consimilitude and an unimpeachable analogy becomes perceptible between the concept of the transcendennal aspect of Lord Śiva elucidated in Śrīkaṇṭhabhāṣya of Siddhānta Śaivāgama school and that of the indefinable monistic Brahman, narrated in several leading upaniṣadas in an etymological complex of Superlatively transcendental connotation. In Tirumantiram composed by the South Indian Śaiva ascetic Tirumulār in Tāmil language both Agamas and Vedas are conceived as the instructions of one and the same Omnific Ultimate Reality.[15] As this text suggests the doctrines of Siddhānta and Vedānta aim at the one and same spiritual realisation although differences are marked in the process of their analyses.[16] Tirumulār divides Śaivism into four different stages from the standpoint of cadre of Spiritual elevations.[17] These four different stages are illustrated as (i) Aśhuddha Śaivism (ii) Śhuddha Śaivism (iii) Mārga Śaivism and (iv) Kaḍumaśhuddha Śaivism.[18] Aśhuddha Śaivism confines itself to the phallic aḍoration in the temple, offerings of cocoanut, scented sticks and flowers to the icon and anicon of Lord Śiva and the observation of elaborate rites and rituals.[19] Śhuddha Śaivism considers Vedānta as pure Śaiva Siddhānta and aims at the realisation of Śaivabrahmajñāna or Wisdom relating to the ultimate reality of Lord Śiva. From the practical standpoint the followers of this Śaivism minimise the ritualistic aspects of reverence although theoretically it discards these aspects completely.[20] In Mārga Śaivism, emphasis is laid upon the realisation of Śaivabrahmajñāna in body, speech and mind and upon the meditation of transcendental Brahman aspect of Lord Śiva.[21] Rites and rituals are disapprobated absolutely in this Śaivism. Kaḍuma-śhuḍdha Śaivism is the final state of Śaivite elevation. In this state, the adherent attains perfect Siddhi. In this State the adherent attains perfect Siddhi and realises spiritual communication of regular nature with Lord Śiva. In this Stage the spiritually elevated adherent is called N-andīn, the immediate attendant of Lord Śiva.[21A] Appara, a contemporary of pallavaking Mahendra-I of Seventh Century A. D. also believes in both the immanent and transcendent aspects of Lord Śiva.[22] In the immanent aspect Śiva figures as one of the Hindu Trinity and extirpates the evil for the healthy continuity of the cosmic order. As Parāpara or Paramajyoti or refulgent Śiva he establishes his indistinct identity with Śakti and descending the earth as a preceptors preaches the Śaivite doctrines for the incoronation of Śivatva or cosmopolitan equity in all Jivas or animate creatures.[23] As the one and only one Stambha or Sthāṇu Śiva Śiva is eternal, illimitable, unintelligible, Omnipresent, Omniscient and omnipotent Ultimate Reality and is beyond all illusive discriminations. He is the one and the only one perpectual source of vital manifestations.[24] In the meditation of transcendent Śiva, body is conceived as temple, mind figures as worshipper, realisation of truth from the curious search of Śivabrahmajñāna is considered as devotional enthusiasm and purity, the spiritual emotion of the heart is treated as phallic emblem or liṇga and love, leaning and loyalty are treated as the ingredient of yogic ritualisation.[25] All these illustrations thus logically suggest that the doctrines of Siddhānta Śaivāgama School were not anti-vedic and anti-vedantic in nature. On the otherhand it had embraced the doctrines of Brahmajijñāsā and non-dualism in the course of its evolution Whatever may be the definition and nature of Siddhānta Śaiva doctrine propounded by Maheśvara, it is possible that the Śaivāgamas continued to propel their evolution in between the period beginning with the composition of Śvetāśvatara Upaniṣad and ranging upto the rise of Madhavacharya in fourteenth century A. D. in both the Northern and Southern India in Sanskrit, prakrit, Tamil, Telugu, Kanadi and other regional languages. The Tamil people consider the Śaivāgamas composed in Southern India in regional languages as pre-vedic Drāviḍian compositions. But as on these Śaivāgamas the influence of the Sanskrit language and upaniṣadic doctrine are traced out conspicuously, reluctance interrupts the recognition of this view. Scholar criticises this view as "a mythical patriotic belief" of its advocates. Dr. S. N. Dasgupta places the dawning era of the composition of these Śaivāgamas to the last part of pre-christian age as he finds the quotations from Sanskrit Śaivāgamas in Brahmasūtra of Bādarāyaṇa.[27] Dr. S. N. Rajguru assigns this age to the age of Kuśhāṇas.[28] From the doctrinal Shadow of Śvetāśvatara upanisada it appears plausible to believe that these Siddhānta Śaivāgama doctrines began to evolve from the last part of the First century B. C. onward. Most possibly the Siddhānta doctrine travelled from Northern India to its Southern part enroute central province and South Kośala.

Mattamayura Saivism is believed to have attained its origin in Northern India in the lap of gradually growing Siddhānta doctrine. The name of the Śaivite Āchārya patangaśiva is found recorded in Dharmal iṇgeśvar copper plates of Devandravarman—I the Eastern Gaṇgaking of Kaliṇga.[29] This Śaivite Āchārya is identified with pataṇgaśambhu described in Bilhari and Ranod Stone inscription.[30] This Śaiva saint was the disciple of Mattamayūra Śaiva recluse Vyomaśiva—I and had initiated Devendravarman—I in Mattamayūra Śaivism In Dharmaliṇgeśvar copper plates.[31] pataṇgaśiva is eulogised as "well-versed in veda, vedāṇga, purāṇa annals, Nyāya and his own Siddhānta doctrines, Vyomaśiva—II or Gaganaśiva praised as an erudite scholar in Śaivasiddhāntas in the karhad Copper plates of Rāṣṭrakūṭa king Kṛishṇa III,[32] in Vāyavīya Samhitā of Śiva purāṇa and Śaivasiddhānta dīpikā of paundit Śambhudeva, Siddhānt Śaiva school is distinguished as a separate sect from pāśupata, Roudra, Jangama, Raseśvara, Ugra, pratyabhijñā and Bhaṭṭa and is treated as Saivāgama Siddhānta school.[33] All these evidences thus clearly assert that the Mattamayūra Śaivism developed as a school of Siddhānta Saivagama Saivism.

Diametrically antithetical views prevail among the scholars with regard to the place of the origin of this Mattamayūra Śaivism. Observing the popularity of this school in central provinces of India in the middle ages scholars demonstrate central India as its birth place.[34] According to the view of this group of Scholars, this school attained increasing popularity in Tripuri of Haihaya kingdom being originated in central India Since a remote antiquity. Few other scholars consider the Rohitak regions near Delhi as the cradle land of this Saivism,[35]

As it has been discussed earlier, the school of Siddhānta Śaivism had possessed a continuity of gradual evolution in Northern India since the days of the composition of śvetāśvataropaniṣad and it is in the lap of this school that the Mattamayūra Śaivism had attained its genesis in Northern India. Like the Siddhānta Śaivite followers, the Mattamayūra Śaivas also equalises Lord Śiva with the Upaniṣadic Brahman who is believed as immanent as also transcendent.[36] Northern India embodying the ancient Āryāvartta was undoubtedly the motherland of Upaniṣadic Brāhmanism. In the Sabhāparvan of Mahābhārata, its author while delineatin the conquest of Nakula records the domiciles of Mattamayūra Kṣhatriya tribes in the Rohitaka regions in the contiguity of Delhi. These Kṣhatriyas fought against the pāṇḍavas and their militia for the autonomy of their lands.[37] keeping in view this suggestion of Mahabharata, Dr. N. K. Sahu, Dr. S. C. Behera and many other historians.[38] theorise that the Mattamayūra Śaivāchāryas hailed from Rohitak region near Delhi and preached their doctrines in Western, eastern and central India in course of their travel to different places. While collecting materials for his thesis 'Sahajayāna in Orissa' in 1982, this author had the opportunity of discussion with late Mr. Dinabandhu Badpanda, a prolific astrologer of the village Pankeldadar near Binka. Sri Badpanda while voicing an analysis on the nature and definition of kala in astrology had expressed few points on Śaivism, antiquity of the linga of the Kapileśvar temple of Charada near Binka and on Mattamayūra Śaivism from an old palm-leaf manuscript called 'Kapileśha-Māhātmya' All his points recited in Sanskrit verses naturally allured me to obtain the manuscript. But inspite of my several approaches at his door, all my attempts ended in fiasco. Late Mr. Panda dropped an iron curtain to my dancing curiousity with his departure from this world. The verses, uttered by Mr. Panda during my discussion are as follows—

> "Vṛindārakairupāsitaṁ Mattamayūrah samjñitaṁ
> Dṛiśhyate Sthāṇuliṇgoyaṁ Kadamba sumabāsitaṁ
> Kurutīrthe Kurukṣhetre Koshavane Manorame
> Asmintīrthe Bhavam dhātvā narah muchyate kilviṣhai"

If at all, these verses are believed to have been impregnated with truth then in will be a fact that the Mattamayūra Śaivism originated in the Koṣhatraya forest of Kurutirtha near Kurukṣhetra with the enshrinement of a linga called Mattamayūra. The Nathas who generally believe the Śaivāgamas based on Siddhānta doctrine as their sacred religious texts assign the nomenclature 'Siddhamata' or "Siddhānta" to their centripetal religious doctrines.[39] They also delineate the beautiful Koṣhatraya forest near Kurukṣhetra as the seat of their primal lord

Śiva, called Ādināth.[40] Lodhia copperplates of Mahasivagupta Balarjuna of the Somaruling dynasty record that the Śaiva ascetic pramathāchārya and his disciple Sulapāṇī had come to South Kośala from the pañchayajña Tapovana of Dvaitavana and had accepted land grants from this king for the regular veneration of Iśāneśvara Śivaliṇga enshirned in a temple of Khadirapadraka in South Kośala.[41] Śaivāchāryas pramatha and Sulapāṇī were the followers of Mattamayūra Śaivism.[42] The village Khadirapadraka of Lodhia copper plate may be identified with village Khairpadar and the village Baidyapadrak of this copper plate may be identified with Banjipadar. Both these villages are located in a reliable proximity from Ranipur Jharial, the most famous cultural centre of Mattamayūra Śaivism of age-old South Kośala. It is revealed from all these discussions that Kurukṣhetra comprising the regions Dvetavana, Rohitaka and other neighbouring regions were the cradle land of Mattamayūra Śaivism and from these regions it spread to mony places through the preachings of the ascetics of this school. Rise of this Śaivism in South Kośala and Orissa became possible most probably because of its travel from these regions enroute central province.

From a remote antiquity Orissa appears to have accorded a popular appreciation to this school of Śaivism. The efflorescence and extension of this Śaivism in North Orissa ancient Kongoda Maṇḍala and South Kośala are proved by many authentic historical testimonies. A comprehensive list of the Mattamayūra Śaivāchārya Tradition becomes available as per the suggestions of the Ranod Stone Inscriptions of King Yaśhovarman and Bilhari stone inscriptions of the chedī kings.[43] The list may be recorded as follows.

Kadambaguhādhivāsin
- Śaṅkhamaṭhikādhipati
  - Terambipāla
    - Āmarddakatīrthanātha Rudraśambhu
      - Mattamayūranātha Purandara
        - Kavachaśiva
          - Sadāśiva
            - Hṛidayaśiva
              - Vyomaśiva
                - Pataṅgaśambhu
        - Dharmaśambhu
          - Sadāśiva
            - Madhumateya Purandara
              - Chudaśiva
                - Hṛidayaśiva II
                  - Aghoraśiva
                - Prabhava śiva
                  - Praśāntaśiva
                    - Iśānaśiva
                      - Gaganaśiva II
                    - Prabodhaśiva

Many of the Śaiva ascetics enlisted in the above Mattamayūra Śaivāchārya Tradition are appeared to have been associated with the Śaivite cultures of Orissa. Kadambaguhādhivāsin Mattamayūra Śaivāchārya means a Mattamayūra Śaiva ascetic who had his abode in a cave called Kadambaguhā. Kadambaguha is identified as Kadwaha in Madhya pradesh by some of the scholars while few other scholars identify it with Kadambagiri of the Rithapur copper plates of Bḥavattavarman.[44] But as in Sanskrit language 'Guhā' means a cave and the ascetics of ancient India used to live in the caves of Mountains, this Kadambaguhā may resonably be identified with the cave of a mountain. Either the locality Kadwaha or the village Kadambagiri can not be identified with Kadambaguhā. Śaṅkhamaṭhi Kādhipati means master of Saṅkhamaṭhika. This maṭhika or maṭha may reasonably be identified with the famous Śaṅkhakāra maṭha of the Asanapat stone Inscriptions of the king Śatrubhanja of Nāga ruling dynasty.[45] This Śaṅkhakāramaṭha was located in Ahichhatraka[46] which is identified with the modern Ramnagar of Bareili district of Uttar Pradesh.[47] As from the palaeographical standpoint the Asanapat Stone Inscriptions are placed in Fourth century A. D. and as in this lithic record Śatrubhanja figures as a donor of abundant charity, it is conclusive that this maṭha had already been established in its glory and grandeur by the fourth century A. D. As in the chandrehe stone inscriptions of Prabodhaśiva, Ranod Stone Inscriptions of Yaśhovarman and Bilhari stone Insctiption of Chedi kings, there are records of prayers of the Naṭarāja countenance of Lord Śiva[48] it is invariably believed that this form of Siva had inspired accumulating popularity among the adherents of Mattamayūra Śaivism. In Mattamayūra Śaiva centre, Ranipur Jharial a Naṭarāja image is found seated in the centre of the yoginī piṭha of this place. In the upper portion of Asanapat stone inscriptions an image of N-aṭaraj Śiva is found inscribed conspicuously. Māntric adoration of lord Śiva is a prominent feature of Mattamayūra Śaivism. For this the Śaivāchāryas of this Śaivite School were not only reciting the Śaiva mantras but were also composing mantras with a meditative perception.[49] Verse XXIII of Ranod Stone Inscriptions record the testimony about the composition of mantra by the ascetics and preceptors of this school.[50] In Asanapat stone inscriptions Śatrubhanja is endowed with the epithets 'Mahārudrasya Chaturbhi yugāntachala Kīrtti' aṇd Lakṣhamantradhāraṇaikadakṣhah'.[51] In significance of his epithet 'Lakṣhamantradhāraṇaikadakṣhah' Śatrubhanja may be described to have been initiated into several mantras. All these facts traceable from the Asanapat stone Inscriptions have much in common with the features of Mattamayūra Śaivism and on these affinities Śatrubhanja, the donor of these inscriptions may reasonably be aceepted as a devotee of Mattamayūra Śaivism. Possibly from the time of Śatrubhanja the king of Vindhyatavi kingdom in Fourth century A. D. the Mattamayūra Śaivism began to exercise its influence on the culture of Ori-sa. Kadambaguhā was most probably a cave in the mountainous region of North India in a reliable nearness with Ahichtraka.

The exact time of the efflorescene of the Mattamayūra Saiva ascetics delineated in the above Mattamayūra Śaivāchārya Tradition is yet a controversial issue in the pages of history. Scholars profess dimetrically opposite view with regard to their time of efflorescene. Although no source-materials become available to upraise the iron curtain of mutual-antithesis among the scholars it appears reasonable to believe that the Saiva ascetics Kadambaguhādhivāsin and Śaṇkhamaṭhikādhipati remained efflorescent in the intervening period from 340 A. D. to 425 A. D. Most possibly Śatrubhañja travelled to Saṇkhakār Matha of Ahichatraka towards the closing years of fourth century A.D. when Kadambaguhādhivāsin had already experienced the separation of his body and soul and his disciple Saṇkhamaṭhikādhipati had risen to prominence. The author is inclned to place the time of Kadambaguhadhivasin from 300 A. D. to 350 A. D. and that of his disciple from 340 A. D. to 425 A. D. The image of a Śaiva saint inscribed at the right hand side of the image of Naṭarāja Śiva on the Asanapāt Stone Inscriptions may be identified with Saṇkhamaṭhikādhipati. The Śaivāchārya Terambipāla succeeded Saṇkhamaṭhikādhipati and may be suggested as an ascetic of fifth century A. D. This Terambipāla who had his maṭha or monastery in Terahi of Madhyapradesh was prominent for preaching this Śaivism in the Central province of India. He most probably lived from 400 A. D. to 480 A. D. Rudraśambhu of Mattamayūra Śaivāchārya Tradition was popularly known as Āmarddakatīrthanātha. The place Āmarddaka Tīrtha is acquainted with Amod in Madhya pradesh by some Scholars, but this identification does not appear reasonable. Āmarddaka Tīrtha is described in the Senakapat stone Inscription of Mahāśivagupta Bālārjuna[52] in Saurastra Haddala copper plate in Saka Era 836 or

914 A. D.[53] and in Rajorgarh Stone Inscriptions[54] of Rajasthan in Vikrama Samvat 1016 or 959 A. D. This Ā-marddaka may be identified with Amarddā in Mayurbhanja district of Orissa. In this Amarddā, the Gaganeśvara Śiva temple was found in a good condition until the Muslim rule in Orissa. The Someśvar temple constructed by Gaganasiva II in Ranipur Jharial displays an inscription on the upper portion of the doorway of Chamber where the Someśvar Linga is found enshrined. In this inscription Śiva is prayed as "Gaganaikastvayaṁ prabhuh".[55] As the word "gagana" denoting sky occurs commonly in Gaganaśiva, Gaganeśvara and in the above-noted inscriptions and as in Mattamayūra, Śaiva theology Lord Ś-iva is conceived as illimitable and Omnipresent as the all-pervading sky the Gaganeśvara Śiva worship in Amardda may be conceived as a product of Mattamayūra Śaiva influence. Most possibly the Śiva temple of Gaganeśvar in Amarddha was built with the effort of Āmarddakatīrthanāth Rudraśambhu in the closing part of fifth century A. D. Rudrasambhu may be believed to have been alive in between 450 A. D. to 500 A. D. The saiva ascetic Mattamayuranatha purandara was the disciple of this Rudrasambhu. It may be believed that purandara assumed the honnrific title "Mattamayūranath" at the time of his initiation to this Śaivism in Amarddā by his preceptor Rudraśambhu. He may be believed to be the founder of Raṇīpadra penance-grove in Ranipur-Jharial in the first-half of Sixth century A. D.[56] In his presiding supervision the Siddheśvar temple in Raṇipadra might have been built with the enshrinement of Liṇga named Siddheśvara Śiva in adherence to the practice of Siddhānta theories. Siddheśvara of Someśvar Temple Inscriptions of Ranipur-Jharial is identified by paundit Kedarnath Mahapatra as Lord Buddha by mistake.[57] On his erroneous identification Mr. Mahapatra has been inclined to acquaint the image of a contemplative ascetic at the door wall of the garbhagriha or the sanctum as the image of Lord Buddha.[57A] As this image is found seated in a meditative pose, as there is the

sign of semicircular moon over the head of this image and the image is found embellished with a sacred thread or Yajnopavita on its body, it is undoubtedly an image of a Śaiva-ascetic within the fold of Orthodox Brahmanism or Vedicism and can in no way be an image of Lord Buddha. As the gesture shown by this image indicates a praying-pose of this image towards Lord Someśvar, it is also not the image of Siddheśvara Siva as narrated in Someśvar Temple Inscriptions. It is undoubtedly the image of a Śaiva Sanyāsī and most probably that of Iśānaśambhu, the preceptor of the architect of this temple. It is possible that Siddheśvar Śiva described in later Someśvar temple Inscriptions was worshipped in this place in a different temple at the centre of this place the remains of which are seen at present at the centre of the huge rockbed of this place. These remains present a dumb witness to the worship of Siddheśvar Śiva in a temple constructed by Mattamayūranātha purandar who most probably travelled from this place to Avantī and initiated the king of Avantī into Mattamayūra Śaivism.[58] He may be believed to have been prominent in the first-half of Sixth century A. D. From this time onward the adoration of Siddhesvar appears to have acquired popularity in this place and centring around his veneration, the tāntric cult of Siddhayogeśvarī Chāmuṇḍā in Seventh. Century A. D. and Siddhi conferring yoginīs evolved in the later part of eight or opening part of the ninth Century A. D. In a corner of this huge rockbed the image of Chāmuṇḍā is found inscribed on a large stone on one siḍe and on the opposite side of this large stone the inscribed images of Saptamātṛikās, Ganeśha and Vīrabhadra are observed clearly. As this chamunda is found seated on a corpse holding in her hand a pot of wine and munching a piece of bone besides other traditional features, as Vīrabharda is marked with a corpse as his vehicle and as in the Yoginī piṭha of this place the yoginīs display poses of exhilarated dancing around the image of N-aṭarāja Śiva it is believed that the Bāmāchārin Tāntric cult was also efflorescent in this place assigning centripetal importance to Lord Siddheśvar. This tāntric trend most probably developed in Ninth century A. D. although the worship of Siddheśvar was established from Sixth century A. D. Mattamayūra Śaiva ascetic, Kavachaśiva, Sadāśiva and Hṛidayaśiva may be confided to have been prominent in this school of Śaivism in the later half of Sixth century A. D. Sadāśiva is believed to have performed his penance in Raṇīpadra or Ranipur-Jharial.[59] Vyomaśiva of the above noted Śaivāchārya Tradition was the disciple of Hṛidayaśiva. He is believed to have ascended to the acme of popularity in the first half of Seventh century A. D. in the penance-grove of Raṇīpadra. His time of consecration to popularity is fixed erroneously by paundit Kedarnath Mahapatra in the periphery of Ninth century A. D.[60] Paundit Guṇaratna and Rājaśekhara suggest the composition of Vyomavatī or Vyomamatī commentary by this Vyomaśiva on the praśastapādabhāṣya of Vaiśheṣika philosophy.[61] The time of the rise of Guṇaratna and Rājaśekhara are generally assigned in tenth century A. D. although a scholar has unreasonably suggested this time as fourteenth century A. D.[62] As the time of Gunaratna and Rājaśekhara does not precede tenth century A. D. it is logical to assign the duration of the composition of vyomavatī and that of the rise of its author before tenth century A. D. But priority to 10th century A. D. does not particularise N-inth century A. D. It may mean any century before tenth century A. D. Paundit Mahapatra, to comprise the time of Vyomavatī as also of its author misinterpretes the word Śhaṇkara in verse 37 of Ranod Stone Inscriptions of king Yaśhovarmā in the significance of Śhaṇkarāchārya. But as this verse is recorded as "Sarvajnah Ṣpuṭameṣha kopi Bhagavān anya kṣhitau Śhaṇkarah"[63] and as the word Ś-haṇkar in this verse is not accompanied either with the prefix of suffix "Āchārya", it is a gross mistake to accept this word as a synonym of Śhaṇkarāchārya of ninth century A. D. in the absence of distinctive particularisation. As this verse suggests Śaivāchārya Vyomaśiva had attained the status of Omni intelligent Lord Śiva because of his yogic perfection. Hence in this verse he is compared with Lord Śiva, and not with Śhaṇkarāchārya of ninth century A. D. and on this reasonable ground it may be asserted that neither he can be called the Second Śhaṇkarāchārya nor be can be placed in Ninth century A. D. Further in the Śhaṇkarabhāṣya Śaivasiddhānta is blamed as anti-upaniṣadic in nature.[64] As Mattamayūra Śaivism is a school of Śaiva Siddhāntas, it must have been blamed by Śhaṇkarāchārya as anti-upanisadic and anti-vedic. On the Vaiśheṣika philosophy, Praśastapāda wrote his commentary in fifth century A. D.[65] According to Ranod Stone Inscription of Yaśhovarman[66] Vyomaśiva elucidated the real defination of Matter having composed Vyomavatī commentary on praśastapādabhāsya. As with the rise of Sun the darkness disappears and the entire world become visible with light, the vyomavati commentary according this inscription removed ignorance and revealed the real definition and nature of matter. Śhaṇkarāchārya refuted the atomism of Vaiśheṣika philosophy.[67] Vyomaśiva a protagonist of Vaiśheṣika philosophy and also its theory of atomism, an exponent in giving the reasonable defination of matter and an advocate of Siddhānta theory must not have been compared with Śhaṇkarāchārya even at a much later date of the exposition of the Ranod inscription. A patron of Vaiśheṣika philosophy, he must not have been compared with Āchārya Shaṇkara an antagonist of that philosophy even at a later date by the Mattamayūra Śaivas. As Vyomaśiva was the preceptor of patangaśambhu who may be identified with patangaśiva of Dharmaliṇgeśvar copper plates of the Eastern Ganga king Devendravarman, it seems logical to believe that Vyomaśiva flourished in first-half of seventh century A. D. and during this period he composed Vyomavatī and several mantras in the penance-grove of Raṇīpadra.[68] With the effort of this eminent recluse, the Mattamayūra Śaivism attained popularity in many parts of Orissa and Madhya pradesh. Dr. S. C. Behera considers the God Śiva invoked and prayed by the Sailodbhava king at the opening of their several charters as Mattamayūra Śiva because in consistence with his suggestion it is observed that Lord Śiva narrated in Buguda copper plates of King Mādhavavarma differs from the paśupata Śiva described in Ṣaḍdarsanasamuchchaya of Āchārya Haribhadra in appearance, attire and ornaments.[69] The features of Śiva delineated in this Buguda copper plates maintain a resemblance with those of Śiva prayed in Khandipada Nuapalli copper plate[70] of Charamparāja Ayaśhobhita-I who flourished in Seventh century A. D. and this Saivism enjoyed royal patronage of the Śailodbhavas most probably owing to the influence of Amarddaka and preaching of the prolific Saivite Scholar Vyomaśiva.

Pataṇgaśambhu in the Mattamayūra Śaivāchārya tradition figures as disciple of Vyomaśiva. According to Dharmaliṇgeśvar copper plates of Devendravarman, the Eastern Gaṇga King of Kaliṇga, he is described as a scholar of Veda, Vedāṇga, Itihāsa, purāṇas and Nyāya and a genius of Siddhānta theories of his school.[71] He according to this charter initiated king Devendravarman into his Śaivism and accepted the village Haḍuvaka in puṣpagiri pānchāli viṣaya as a charity in lieu of his initiation from this king.[71A] From the land-grant that he received, he donated half of the area of lands for the worship of Yogeśvaraśiva and the residue to his disciples and thus maintained the lofty ideal of Indian asceticism in a conspicuous sincerity.[72] His disciples as it is known from this charter lived happily in Kaliṇga accepting these gifts with the pleasure of their preceptor[73] and became helpful in promoting the cause of Mattamayūra Śaivism. This pataṇgaśiva is identified with pataṇgaśambhu of Mattamayūra Śaivāchārya tradition.[74] Dharmaliṇgeśvar copper plates were issued in Gaṇga Era 184 which may correspond to the christian year 682 A. D.[75] Pataṇgaśambhu or pataṇgaśiva also played active role in spreading this Śaivism in Koṇgodamaṇḍala Mahāśivagupta Bālārjuna the Somavaṁśī king of South Kośala was also a devoted patron of this Śaivism. He began his rule in South Kośala in the last phase of eighth century A. D.[76] In his 57th year of his reign he issued his Lodhia copper plates.[77] According to this copper plate inscription, Acharya Śūlpāṇī come of South Kośala from 'Panchayajna penancegrove of Dvaitavana near Delhi and Kurukṣhetra region and accepted land grant for the worship of Iśāneśvar Śiva enshrined in a temple of Khadirapadraka.[77A] The villages vaidyapadraka and Khadirapadraka narrated in this copper plate may be identified with Vanjipadar and Khairpadar near Raṇīpadra or Ranipur Jharial. Śūlapāṇī also seems to have played a significant role in spreading Mattamayūra Śaivism in South Kośala. The Senakapat Inscriptions of Mahāśivagupta Bālājuna while recording a graphic description of the dancing of N-aṭarāja Śiva also suggest the advent of Sadāśivāchārya from Āmarddaka to South Kośala.[78] As Āmaddaraka played a vital role for disseminating Mattamayūra Śaiva culture this Sadāśiva is also believed as a Mattamayūra Śaiva sage. From the standpoint of historical chronology this sadāśiva seems different from the Śaiva saint of consemblent nomenclature in Mattamayūra Śaivāchārya Tradition. The role of this Śaiva ascetic is also worth accountable for the growth of this Śaivism in South Kośala.

On the huge rocked of Ranipur Jharial the Somesvar temple stands in the midst of Indralāṭh Brick temple, yoginīpīṭha and a number petty temples of different sizes It amplifies a lot on the age-old Mattamayūra Śaiva importance of this place preserving an inscription in the upper wall of the entrance of its sanctum or garbhagriha. This inscription bears a testimony[79] that this temple was constructed by Śaivāchārya Gaganaśiva who came to this place from Uttara Teramba.[80] By the time of his arrival to this place, it had already been a Tīrtha of consecrated popularity.[81A] place to attain the elevated status of a Tīrtha needs indispensable a prolonged cultural background of several centuries added by a popular appreciating of unquestionable continuity. As Rome is not built in a day so also a Tīrtha in religious culture. On this axiom it is desirable that the antiquity of this place should be analysed keeping in view a critical appreciation of its different religious growth and not alone the inscription in question and faint occurances of the activities of Gaganaśiva in this place in this lithic record. As this inscription suggests clearly this place was a sacred shrine of the worship Siddheśvar, Somasvāmī, Lakṣhmī and many other deities much before the advent of Gaganaśiva to this place. This saint magnified this trend of the multilateral adorations of this place by building a temple of Someśvar by preaching and by adding something to its continued popularity. Paundit K. N. Mahapatra appears to have misinterpreted the terms Siddheśvara, Somasvāmī and Lakshmī of this inscription. He explains Siddheśvara as Buddha, Lakshmī as Gajalakshmī and dividing the word Somasvāmī as Soma Svāmī interpretes Soma as Someśvara and Svāmī as Kārttikeya the son of Śiva.[82] Advocating the worship of all these deities within the precinct of Somaśvara temple, he identifies the image of a Śaiva ascetic at the entrance wall of Garbhagṛiha of this temple as Buddha.[83] Lakṣhmī as Gajalakṣhmī found on the lintel of this Grabhagṛiha and Soma as Someśvara liṇga enshrined in this Garbhagṛiha.[84] He observes silence in identifying Svāmī because of the untraceability of Kārttikeya image in this temple. The view of Paundit Mahapatra is accompanied with many misconceptions. An unbiased perusal of this inscription reveals that somasvāmī of this record is the Someśvar Śiva liṇga worshipped in the garbhagriha of this temple. This linga was worshipped even berore Gaganaśiva who simply constructed a temple to add to this worship an institutional importance. Siddheśvar of this inscription was most probably Siddheśvar Sivalinga which was adored in a separate temple in the place at the centre of its huge rockbed. The remains of the stone-cluster and the sign of the desecrated plinth found at the centre of this place are the tacit testimonies of this suggestion. The cult of Chāmuṇḍā and the sixty-four yoginīs developed in this place centring around the veneration of Siddheśvara. The image of Śaiva ascetic which is identified by mistake as Buddha by paundit Mahapatra[85] is neither Buddha nor Siddheśvara Śiva. It is not Buddha because it displays the emblem of half-moon or Ardhachandra at its head and decoration of sacred thread from its choulder to its belly. It is also not the image of Siddheśvara śiva because the iconographical features of this Siva are not found in this image and it is also not justifiable that one form of Siva would be seen praying another form of Śiva in ideas of a sculptor. It is most probably the image of Iśānaśiva or Iśānaśambhu the preceptor of Gaganaśiva and this image has been inscribed here most probably with the instruction of Gaganaśiva as a token of his reverence towards his preceptor. Siddheśvara Śiva was most probably worshipped in Ranipur Jharilal in a separate temple since the time of Mattamayūranatha purandara as the presiding deity of Siddhānta Tattvas or theories. Lakshmī of Someśvar Temple Inscription was most probably not the image of Gajalakṣhmī found on the door jamb of the sanctum of this temple. In the temple architecture of Orissa Gajalakṣhmī figures as a decorative motif of many Saiva temples and she does not figure as cult-deity or deity of reverential importance especially in these Śaiva temples. In the Devīmāhātmya Section of Mārkaṇḍeya purāṇa which is generally named as Śrīdurgā Saptaśhati, Durga is described as Lakshmī in many places[86] In this text chāmuṇḍā is depicted as "primal Sakti Mahālakṣhmī" ie. as Sarvasyādyā Mahālakṣhmīh Trīguṇā parameśvarī.[87] In the Tāntric adoration of Śrīdurgā Saptaśhati Durgē is worshipped in her three aspects which are named as Mahākālī, Mahālakṣhmī and Mahāsarasvatī. Siddheśvarī Chāmuṇḍā worshipped as the consort of Siddheśvara Śiva in Ranipur-Jharial has most probably been recorded as Lakṣhmī in this inscription in consonance with the Śāktaist conceptualisation of Devī Māhātmya. The Devī-Māhātmya section of the Mārkaṇḍeya purāṇa is an interpolation of Sixth century A. D. to this purāṇa of fourth century A. D.[87A] The image of Siddheśvarī chāmuṇḍā in Ranipur-Jharial was most probably a sculpture of Seventh century A. D. Centring around the cult of Siddheśvar Siva and Siddheśvarī chāmuṇḍā the Tantric worship of Siddhi-conferring Yoginī began in Ranipur Jharial in the latter part of eighth century A. D.

Kedarnath Mahapatra identifies Ranipur-Jharial as Soma-tīrtha basing his observation on few doubtful verses quoted in Kṛityakalpataru of paundit Lakṣhmīdhar Bhaṭṭa.[88] These verses are quoted from Vāmana purāṇa.[88A] In these verses the descriptive identity of Soma Tīrtha is given with reference to few points. The points as recorded are that the Somatirth is located towards the north of mountain Mahendra a seat of worship of Śambhu and Gopāla and has a tank called Soma-śhitala.[88B] Except these points, these verses do not say anything on Ranipur-Jharial nor on Someśvara nor any other distinctive feature for which one should be inclined to identify this Somatīrtha with Ranipur-Jharial. On the other hand V mana purāṇa clearly describes that Somatīrtha was located on the bank of river Sarasvatī.[89] All these illustrations thus make it clear that it is a gross mistake to identify Ranipur-Jharial as Somatīrtha. It is a matter of regret that several scholars follow blindly paundit Mahapatra without scrutinising the suggestion of this learned scholar with original source. It is probable that Ranipur-Jharial was Someśvara Liṇga Ādipīṭha or Ādī yoginī Tīrtha as it is iadicated in yogini Tantra.[89A]

Gaganaśiva came to Ranipur-Jharial from Uttara Teramba. This Uttara Teramba is variably identified by scholars with various different places. Paundit Kedarnath Mahapatra analogises this place with Terahi of Madhya pradesh.[90] Dr. N. K. Sahu identifies it with Temra on the bank of rivulet Tong near Ranipur-Jharial asserting Terambi of Ranod inscription and Uttara Teramba of Someśvar temple Incription as one and the same place.[91] Dr. J. K. Sahu differentiating these two places of these two different inscriptions identifies Terambi of Ranod inscription as Terahi and Uttara Teramba of Someśvar Temple inscription as Temra.[92] According to both Dr. Sahu Temra is located to the north of Ranipur Jharial.[93] A critical appreciation of the text of Someśvar Temple Inscriptions leaves an impression that the term Uttara in Uttara Teramba of this inscription is not a term signifying a direction. In Sanskrit Uttara does not mean north alone. It also signifies 'later' or 'subsequent period'. Uttara Teramba here signifies a new Teramba built on commemoration of past or prior Teramba. Most probably this Uttara Teramba grew in new vigour in the contiguity of and in the commemoration of the lofty cultural heritage of purva or prior Teramba. In a distance of five miles from Terahi, a Hindu monastery with the remains of fourteen dilapidated and damaged temples are found in a village called Kadwaha in M. P. These dilapidated temples represent in their relics an architectural style of 10th and 11th century A. D.[94] Most possibly this desolate shrine of Kadwaha was a later growth in reminiscences of the cultural glory of previous Terambi and the growth of Mattamayūra Śaiva culture of this place was subjected to the lofty cultural influence of purva Terambi. This place was most probably recorded by Gaganaśiva as Uttara Teramba in the inscription of his own-built temple. Because Kadambaguhā signifies a cave and is believed to have been located in a reliable nearness with Śaṇkhamaṭha or Śaṇkhakāramaṭha, Kadwaha can in no way be accepted as Kadambaguhā. As Temra near Ranipur Jharial does not possess any archaeological remains and is located towards the east-southern corner, it can not be accepted as

Uttara-Teramba. From Kadwaha or Uttara Temba Gaganaśiva seems to have come to Ranipur-Jharial.

As it is known from the Karhāḍ grant of Rāṣṭrakūṭa king Kṛishna III Gaganaśiva was a scholar of all Śaivasiddhāntas a successful practitioner of penance and a disciple of Iśāna-Śambhu.[95] He is also described to have accepted charity from this king in this record.[96] The date of this grant is 880 Saka year or 958 A. D. From the palaeographical stand-point the Somesvar Temple Inscription is dated back to tenth century A. D.[97] The architectual style of Somesvar Temple is also assigned to tenth century A. D. All these corelations of facts however make it logical to believe that Gaganasiva came from Kadwaha or Uttar Terambi to Ranipur Jharial in 10th century A. D. and built the Somesvar temple in this place in that century. He added further vigour to the popularity of this place as also of his Saivism by encouraging the continuity of the cult of Somesvar, Siddhesvar and Siddhesvari chamunda of this place. He also became instrumental in popularising his Saivism in the Barkuru region of South Kanada and as such his name is found in a ston inscription of Somesvar temple at Barkuru.[98] All these illustrations however make it clear that although Gaganasiva flourished as a Saivacharya in Uttara Teramba or Kadwaha in the primary stage of his initiation he travelled to several places of India for preaching and popularising Mattamayura Saivism. His role for elevating this Saivism are traced in Madhyapradesh, Orissa, Maharastra and South Kanada, He was not the author of Vyomavatī commentary as few scholars have wrongly misconceived him. This Śaivāchārya lived from 920-995 A. D. Probably.

All the above discussions thus suggest that Mattamayūra Śaivism developed in Orissa from Fourth to Eleventh century A. D. Although the list of Mattamayūra Śaivāchārya Tradition have been available with its pertinent inscriptions from

Madhya Pradesh, the Saints of this Śaivism established their religious centres from the Himālayān region of North India to Kanada region of South India. In Orissa, this Saivism had been popular in Kaliṇga, Koṇgoda and South Kośala portions under the patronage of Various royal dynasties of the different ages. Although difference of opinion prevails among the scholars with regard to the identification of Āmarddaka, Raṇīpadra and many other Mattamayūra Śaiva sites reasonability becomes more favourable to the identity of Śaṇkhamaṭha with Śaṇkha-kāra maṭha of Ahichatra, of Terambi with Terahi of M. P. of Āmarddaka with Amarddā in Orissa, of Raṇipadra with Ranipur Jharial in Orissa and of Uttara Teramba with Kadwaha in M. P.

Mattamayūra Śaivism evolved in the lap of Siddhānta Śaivism. In Śaiva Siddhānta, Trīpadārtha Tattva or Triple matter theories and chatuṣpāda Tattva or four media Therories are considered as the base principles of this Śaivism.[99] Pati Paśu and Pāśa are conceived as three matters of Śaiva Siddhānta. In the traditional interpretation of this Siddhānta doctrine paramaśiva is believed as the pati or master of entire cosmos.[100] He is independent, eternal, almighty of unfailing will and both transcendent and immanent[101] simultaneously. He is immortal and beyond the limitation of vitality since an unintelligible antiquity. Although He is an indefinable and illimitable Śunya or Void,[102] He is not a sonorous nihilism, a negative abyss or an insignificant negativism. He has His extra-ordinary physical manifestation which is not subject to Māyā or illusion, Moha or fetters, Mala or Pollution and other Bhavavikalpas or wordly limitation like Karmavandhana or attachment of action.[103] His physical manifestation is perpetual and beyond decay and destruction.[104] His indefinable and extra-ordinary divine body is an aggregate of five māntric powers or Panchamantraśakti.[105] These five māntric powers are—(i) Iśānā (ii) Tatpuruṣa (iii)

Aghora (iv) Vāmadeva and (v) Sadyojāta.[106] Iśāna is the head of this divine body, Tatpuruṣa is its face, Aghora is its heart, Vāmadeva is its secret part and Sadyojāta is its legs and feet.[107] The Iśāna māntric power of paramaśiva displays compassion and grace to the devotee, Tatpuruṣa gives perfection in acquiring miraculous power like astonishing appearance or disappearance at any moment any at place, Aghora enables paramaśiva for ādāna—Lakṣhaṇa or causing deluge or desecration, Vāmadeva becomes instrumental in preserving the creation and Sadyojāta enforces the creativity of all and every phenomena of the Universe.[108] These five function by these five mantra Śaktis are named as Anugraha, Tirobhāva, Ādāna Lakṣhaṇa, Sthiti-Lakṣhaṇa and Udbhava-Lakṣhaṇa and are in combination called as Panchakṛityas or Five functions.[109] In the Sādhanā or practical realisation of these mantras, Māntrist or the practitioner of Mantras, Mantreśvara or the presiding deity of the mantra, paramaśiva or the supremest God of Mattamayūra Śaivas and the mantra that is practised by the māntrist are all called Śiva and are classed as ingredients of the pati-Tāttvika padārtha or matters of pati-class.[110]

In Śaiva philosophy all Jivātmans are classed as paśu.[111] As this Jivatman vitalises all the limbs of the Body as an indweller in subtle form it is also called Aṇu or neucleus of vitality.[112] It is also named Kṣhetrajna as it remains attached to the body being shrouded by illusion fetters and defilement. Body formed with various elements of Nature is called Kṣhetra in this philosophy. Jivatman achieves spiritual knowledge and power of spiritual elevation when it is liberated from mundane fetters, contamination and sins and begins to rise towards Śivatva or the condition of a Muktātma Śiva or free-soul Śiva. Jiva emancipated from all the worldly defilements becomes Muktātma śiva.[113] This Muktātma Śiva can not be spiritually independent and all-powerful like paramaśiva even though he acquires Śivatva.[114] He remains subordinate, dependent and subject to the mercy of paramaśiva who is eternal omnipresent, and Omnipotent.[115] Jivātman called paśu is divided into three grade from the standpoint of spiritual development. They are called (1) Vijñānākala (2) Pralayākala and (3) Sakala.[116]

The human emotions which increase attachment for corporeal body and spiritual ignorance is called Kalā.[117] Jivātman co-existing with all these Kalās is called Sakala. From the Standpoint of fluctuation of material attachments Sakala Jiva is of two types viz (i) Pakvakaluṣa Jiva and (ii) Apakvakaluṣa Jiva.[118]

Apakvakaluṣa Jiva is the spiritually ignorant Jiva. This Jiva remains unconscious towards all spiritual wisdom being subjected to illusions, fetters and defilements. It suffers from the reaction of attachments and enjoys happiness as per the natural results of its own action.[119] It is lowest grade of its paśusattā or enimal existence.

The pakvakaluṣa Jiva is little bit progressive than Apakvakaluṣa Jiva. Although this jiva is fetter-bound it become capable of imbibing the mercy of paramaśiva being advised by a well qualified Śaiva Teacher for enthusiasm and attempt towards the acquisition of Śaiva Wisdom. In this stage Jiva is respected as Mantreśvara having learnt and adopted the application of several mantras figuring upto one hundred and eighteen.[120]

The pralayākala Jiva excels all Sakala Jiva in spiritual progress. When the Sakalajivas are subjected to Māyā (illusion) Moha (fetters) Mala (defilement) and Karmavandhana (attachment of Karma) the pralayākala Jiva remains chained by Mala and Karmavandhana only.[121] As thematerial attachments of this Jiva are diminished it is called pralayākala Jiva.[122] This jiva is of two types (i) Pakvapāsha pralayākalajiva and

Apakvapāśhapralayākalajiva from the standpoint of variation in spiritual progress.[123] The pakvapāśapralayākala jiva being more progressive among the two is more enlightened than the Sakala and Apakvapāśa pralayākala jiva.[124] It advances to the higher stage of spiritual realisation having lessened the material attachment more than its lower jivas.[125] The Apakvapāśapralayākala Jiva is inferior to Pakvapāśapralayākala Jiva although it is superior to Sakala Jivas in spiritual advancement.[126] As the material attachment of Apakvapāśhapralayākala Jiva is more firm than the other pralayākala jiva it moves in life cycle of birth and death accompanied by paryuṣtaka bitterly then the latter one. Paryustaka according to a group of Śaiva Scholars is described as the combination of panchamahābhuta, panchatanmātrā, panchajnānendriyas, Panchakarmendriyas Saptakalās and Trī-antahkaraṇas while another group of Śaiva philosophers narrates it as the collection of Śabda (sound) Ṣparśa (touch) Rupa (physical appearance) Rasa (fluid of Vitality) Gandha (smell) Buddhi (intelligence) Mana mental proclivities and Ahaṇkāra (self-attachment).[127]

Vijnānākala jivas are more enlightened than all types of Sakala and pralayākalajivas.[128] This jiva displays a systematic comprehension of Śiva-brahma-Jñāna or the Omnitic Reality in paramaśiva and enables itself to transend the material attachments, Karmavandhana or fruits of activities and the qualities or Kalā of corporeal inclination. For this it is called Vijñānākala Jiva. This jiva is also of two Categories (i) Asamātakaluṣa Vijñānākala jiva and (ii) Samāpta kaluṣa Vijñānākala Jiva.[129] Among these two, the first category of jiva displays a fasnt leaning towards defilement although it transcends Māyā, Karma Vandhana and Moha. As it is subject to a faint leaning towards defilement its impurities are not completely removed. So it is termed Asamāptakaluṣavijnanakala Jiva.[129A]

The stage of the Samāptakaluṣa-Vijñānākala Jiva is the culminating stage in the acquirement of Śivatva. In this stage, Jiva is free from all impurities, contamination, attachments and fetters. This Śivatva gives Jiva unquesitonable Astavidyeśvara or master of eight vidyās. The Aṣta Vidyās are explained as (1) Ananta (2) Sūkṣhma (3) Sivottama (4) Ekanetra (5) Ekarudra (6) Trīmurttika (7) Śrī-khanda and Śikhaṇḍīn.[130] The Samāptakaluṣa-Vijñānākala Jiva is considered as Muktātmaśiva or Śiva with free soul.

The Muktātma Śiva relies on the grace and compassion of paramaśiva although impurities and command over Aṣṭavidyā or eight supreme branches of Knowledge.[131] He can not become independent, almighty, eternal and Omnific like paramaśiva.[132] So Śivatva in this Śaivism denotes liberation from fetters, impurities and illusion and incorporates full spiritual development and realisation of the status of Aṣṭavidyeśvara as its positive features.[133] In this stage even, Jiva remains dependent and subordinate to paramaśiva.

From the standpoint of Māyā or illusion, Mala or defilement, Karmavandhana or attachment of deeds and rodhaśakti or force of circumstancial obstacle, Saivism enumerates[135] four bondages or paśas They are Māyā, Mala, Karma and rodhaśakti. Maya illudes the Jiva causing its allurement towards worldly pleasures. Māyā is[135] defined as Parākṛiti or Prakṛiti in whose lap the phenomenal world remains concealed during the deluge and assumes its physical manifestation at the time of regeneration or Sṛiṣhṭi. Māyā is the root cause of all human proclivities. The Śaivas are advised to get rid of it by detachment.[136] All the dishonest mentations are called malas. As unthrashed paddy hides the rice within and the rust, the dazzling of copper pot so dishonest mentation conceals the spiritual potentiality of soul. All dishonest mentations are also called pravṛiṇiśha which means mala. Attachment of deeds is another bondage. Its intensity creates hurdles on the spiritual path having defiled the ideals of sacrifice of the power of the righteous action.[137] Rodhaśakti means[138] innate force. The innate force of water is downward flow, forcible current and coolness. This force of fire is all consuming efficiency, heat and lusture. Like these the rodhaśakti of Kāma or sexual proclivity is excitement, of moha or fascination is imbalancing the concentration, of Krodha or anger is instablising the mind and creating injury to others etc. etc. Because the emotions and qualities of human being have each a rodhaśakti of its own and interacts in day-to-day life, the spiritual potentiality of the soul or Jiva is disturbed and dominated. This obstructs advance on spiritual path. Constant meditation accompanied with a detachment from its results makes mind serene and the rodhasaktis are pacified causing towards a spiritual elevation its positive and auspicious activities. Four media or Chatuṣpāda theory helps a Śaiva to attain Śivatva when all its instructions are set into action properly. The four medias are[139] Vidyā, Kriyā, Charyās and Yoga. By the cultivation of Vidyā ignorance reiterating mundane affliations are removed and the Triple matters theories of eternal value are understood. By Kriyā the māntric powers are owned and discipline, restraints and a meditative ability for spiritual rise are acquired. Caryā gives regularity, austere resolution for spiritual progress and an isolating attitude towards dishonest mentation and activities. Yoga enables for meditation concentration and inauguration of the mystery of the Ṣhaṭ Chakra yoga comprising the yogic advancement through the plexuses of Mūlādhāra, Svādhiṣṭhāna, Maṇipuraka Anāhata, Viśuddha and Sahasrāra. This yogic advance in its successful culmination emancipates soul from all impurities and the Śaiva adherent achieves Siddhi and becomes free soul-Śiva.

Mattamayura Saivism prohibits ciiticism against Śivas, Śaivas, Śaivāchāra and paramaśive. It accepts Non-Violence as base-principle. Even causing distress in any body's mind is a sin in this religion. Although in this Śaivism Paramaśiva is transcendent and immanent and in His latter aspect has a body of Extra-ordinary composition and characteristics the Śaivas of this school worship liṇgas, Śiva images, pārvatī, phanīs or Nāga images and other Śaivite images. They worship popularly also the Naṭarāja aspect of Lord Śiva.

This Śaivism discards all immoralities. Saivas are advised to renounce leanings towards sensual pleasures. The Mattamayūra Āchāryas refrain themselves from the company of woman[140] and observes Brahmacharyas. The Śaivas of this sect establishes temple of Lord Śiva and Śaiva Bihāras for the discourses of different branches of learning. This Śaivism was popular in many parts of India and many royal dynasties accorded patronage to it. Religious centres of this Śaivism are found in Ahichatra, Madhyapradesh, Ellora, Badami, Maharastra, Kongoda, Kalinga, South Kosala, Gurgi and so many places. This Śaivism also displays a liberal tendency and a sense of remarkable assimilative toleration. In many of the religious centres of this Saivism efflorescene of various religious sects are seen in a singular premise. In Ranipur Jharial rise of Śaivism, Vaiṣhṇavism, Śāktaism, Tāntricism, Buddhism and other religious cults are found and believed to have developed in peaceful co-existence. This Śaivism seems to have bequeathed to Orissa a legacy of Unique assimilative toleration and an attitude of amicable synthesis for counteracting the turnado of sectarian fanaticism.

The culture of the cult of Lord Jagannath the peaceful co-existence of Saivism and Vaisnavism in Bhubanesvar, Gandharadi and many other places of Orissa and Liberal attitude of the people of Orissa towards all religions are more or less seemed to have been influenced by this Śaivism.

REFERENCES

1. Gunaratna's Commentary on Haribhadras' Saḍdarśana Samuccaya (Suali Edition calcutta 1905) p. 51.
2. S. N. Dasgupta—A history of Indian Philosophy (Motilal Banarsidass Delhi 1975) Vol. V. p. 14.
3. U. S. Sharma—The Sarvadarśana Saṁgrha of Mādhvāchārya (Choukhamba vidya Bhavan Baranasi 1964. pp. 297-390. Chap. VI. to IX).
4. Ibid—p. 320.
5. and
6. Dr. S. N. Dasgupta—A history of Indian philosophy Vol. V. pp. 15 and 70.
7. Sivadharmottara quoted in Śiva-Jnāna-Siddhi (Oriental Research Institute Baroda. M. S. No, 3726) F. 3.

8 & 9. Dr. S. N. Dasgupta—A history of Indian philosophy. Vol. V. p. 66. Third paragraph and also p. 70.

10. J. L. Sastri—Ancient Indian Tradition and Mythology Śiva purāṇ (Motilal Banarsidass Delhi 1974-1978) Vāyavīyasaṁhitā section—I p. 1788. Chap. V. verses 4-8.
11. Ibid—p. 1789 Chap. V. verse 17. p. 1790. Chap. V. verse 30 1796. Chap. V. verse 33.
12. Śvetaśvetāra Upaniṣad Chap. IV. verse 10.
13. Dr. S. N. Dasgupta—A history of Indian philosophy Vol. V. p. 70. f. n. 2 (Vāyavīya saṁhitā quoted).
14. Ibid—p. 70.
15. Ed. R. C. Majumdar and other—The History and culture of the Indian people—The classical Age (Bharatiya Vidya Bhawan, Bombay—Third Edition 1970). p. 433.
16. Ibid.

17 & 18. Ibid—p. 33.

19, 20, 21 & 21A. Ibid—p. 433.

22. Ibid—pp. 435-436.
23. Ibid—p. 436.
24. Ibid—p. 436.
25. Ibid—p. 436.

26. Dr. S. N. Dasgupta—A history of Indian Philosophy Vol. V. p. 18.
27. Ibid—p. 70.
28. S. N. Rajaguru—Invocatory verses from Inscription Vol. II. (Sarada press 1973) Introduction p. XXVIII.
29. Epigraphia India—XXVI. pp. 62-65.
30. Indian historical quarterly Vol. XXVI. No. 1. pp. 1-16. Orissa Historical Research Journal Vol. II. pp. 275-276.
31. Epigraphia Indica XXVI. p. 62-65.
32. Epigraphia India Vol. V. pp. 278-290.
33. R. G. Bhandarkar—Vaiṣṇavism, Śaivism and Minor Religious System (Indological Book House Varanasi 1965) pp. 126-127.
34. Ed. Dr. M.N. Das—Sidelights on history and culture of Orissa (Vidyapuri Cuttack 1977) p. 327. (View of V. V. Mirashi quoted).
35. Dr. N. K. Sahu—Oḍiā Jātira Itihāsa (In oriya) Part. I. (The Orissa Text Bureau Bhubaneswar 1977) p. 343. Dr. S. C. Behera—Rise and fall of the Śailodbhavas (Punthi Pustik Calcutta 1982) p. 173.
36. Epigraphic Indica. Vol. XXIV. p. 239. Dr. S. C. Behera—Rise and fall of the Śailodbhavas. pp. 169-175,
37. Ed. V. S. Sukanthakar and others—Mahābhārata. The Sabhāparvan Chap. 29. verse 4. (Bhandarkar Oriental Research Institute poona 1944) Ed. Vettam Muni-Purānic Encyclopaedia Motilal Banarsidass Delhi 1979) p. 494.
38. Dr. N. K. Sahu—Oḍiā Jātira Itihāsa part I. p. 343. Dr. S. C. Behera—Rise and Fall of the Sailodbhavas. p. 173.
39. Purnanathji—Gorakṣha Siddhānta Saṁgraha (In Hindi) p. 151.
and
40. (Tantra Mahārnava Quoted) and pages 37-39.
41. Epigraphia Indica—Vol. XXVII. pp. 319-325.
42. Dr. N. K. Sahu—Oḍiā Jātira Itihāsa part I. pp. 343-344.
43. Orissa Historical Research Journal Vol. III. No. 2 September 1954. p. 69. Indian Historical quarterly Vol. XXVI. No. 1. page 1-16.
44. Orissa Historical Research Journal Vol. III. No. 2 Sept. 1954. p. 66. Dr. N. K. Sahu—Oḍiā Jātira Itihāsa part I. pp. 341-342.
45. Dr. S. N. Rajaguru—Oḍiśhāra Itihāsa part—I. Grantha Mandir

Cuttack 1985. p. 278. Parishista—(Kha) In Oriya language. Orissa Historical Research Journal Vol. XIII. No. 2 pp. 1-8. (Asanapat—Stone Inscription Edited).

46. Ibid—(both).

47. Ed. Dr. R. C. Majumdar and others—The History and culture of the Indian people The classical Age p. 8.

48. Epigraphia Indica Vol. XXI. p. 149. Vol. I. pp. 354-355 and also Vol. I. p. 254.

49. Epigraphia Indica—Vol. I. pp. 351-356 Verse 23 of Ranod.

50. stone Inscription.

51. S. N. Rajaguru—Oḍiṣhāra It ihāsa Part—I. p. 278, Parishista (Kha)

52. Epigraphia Indica Vol. XXXI pp. 31-36.

53, Indian Antiquary Vol. XII. pp. 190 ff.

54. Epigraphia Indica Vol. III. pp. 266 ff.

55. Epigraphia Indica Vol. XXIV. p. 239.

56. Epigraphia Indica Vol. I. pp. 351-356. Ranod Stone Inscription verse 15.

57. Orissa Historical Research Journal Vol. III No. 2 September 1954 p. 71.

57A. Ibid.

58. Dr. S. C. Behera Rise and fall of the Śailodbhavas. p. 172. foot note 60.

59, Epirgrphia India Vol. I. pp. 351-356 Ranod Stone inscription Verse. 17.

60. Orissa Historical Research Journal Vol. III. No. 2 September 1954. p. 68.

61. Indian Historical quarterly Vol. X. 1974. p. 165.

62. Dr. S. N. Dasgupta—A history of Indian philosophy Vol. V. pp. 8 and 15. Kavyamimamsa (G. O. S. Baroda) No. 1. p. Introduction XXXI.

63. Epigraphia Indica Vol. I. pp. 351-356 Verse 37 of Ranod Stone inscription quoted by Pt. K. N. Mahapatra in Orissa Historical Research Journal Vol. III. No. 2 September 1954. p. 68.

64. Dr. S. N. Dasgupta—A history of Indian Philosophy Vol. V. p. 70.
65. A.L. Basham—The wonder that was Indian (Sidgwick and Jackson London 1969). p. 326.
66. Epigraphia Indica Vol. I. pp. 351-356 Ranod Stone Inscription Verse 23.
67. A. L. Basham—The wonder that was India. p. 499.
68. Epigraphia Indica Vol. I. pp. 351-356 Verses 23 and 32 of Ranod Stone Inscriptions.
69. Dr. S.C. Behera—Rise and fall of the Śailodbhavas. pp. 169-175.
70. S. N. Rajguru—Inscription of Orissa (Sarada press, Bhubaneswar 1960). Vol. II. Pate 323-326 Lines 1-9 in page 325.
71. Ibid. Pages 70-71.
    Epigraphia Indica Vol. XXVI. pp. 62-65.

71A. Ibid.

72. Ibid.
73. Ibid.
74. See foot note 43 of this essay also the list of Mattamayūra Śaivāchārya Tradition.
75. Epigraphia Indica Vol. XXVI. p · 62-64 S.N. Rajguru-Inscriptions of Orissa Vol. II. pp. 69-71.
76. S.N. Rajaguru—Inscriptions of Orissa Vol. IV. (Sarada Press, Bhubaneswar 1966). p. 354.
77. Epigraphia Indica Vol. XXVII. pp. 319-325.

77A. Ibid.

78. Epigraphia Indica Vol. XXXI. pp, 31-36 verses I and 17.
79. Epigraphia Indica Vol. XXIV. pp. 239.
    Inscriptions of Gaganasiva in Somesvar temple of Ranipur Jharial.
80. Ibid.
81. Ibid.
82. Orissa Historical Research Journal Vol. III. No. 2. September 1954. p, 71.
83. Ibid.
84. Ibid.
85. Ibid.
86. Ed. Ram Narayan Dattasastri—Śrī Durgāsaptaśhati (Gita Press, Gorakhpur Sa mvat 2029) p. 72. Verse 79. p. 98 verse. 5. page 163. verse 22 etc. etc.

87. Ibid. p. 192 verse 4.

87A. Prof. M. Winternitz—A History of Indian literature (Munshiram Manoharlal New Delhi 1972). Volume—I Secon Edition page 565.

88. Orissa Historical Research Journal Vol. III. No. 12 Sept. 1954. p. 72-73.

88. Ibid. Kośala Baktṛitāmālā—First lecture 1977. (DAV College, Titilagarh) Page. 17.

88B. Ibid.

89. A. S. Gupta—The Vāmana purāṇa (All India Kashiraj Trust Varanasi 1968). Sara Māhātmya Section chap—20 verse 4.

89A. Dr. R. P. Mishra—Fragments of Indian culture. Chap—III. and V.

90. Orissa Historical Research Journal Vo. III. No. 2 Sept. 1954. p. 66.

91. Dr. N. K. Sahu Oḍiā Jātira Itihāsa Part—I. page 342.

92. Ed. M. N. Das—Sidelights on History and culture of Orissa. p. 332, (View of Dr. Sahu in hisarticle.)

93. See the text vide above noted foot notes No. 91 and 92.

94. Orissa Historical Research Journal Vol. III. No. 2. Sept. 1954. p. 66. (view of Gavde quoted).

95. Epigraphia Indica Vol. IV. pp. 278-290.

96. R. G. Bhandarkar—Vaiṣṇavism, Śaivism and Minor Religious systems. p. 118.

97. Dr. Chabra places the script of the Inscription in tentheleventh century A. D. in Epigraphia Indica Vol. XXIV. pp. 239-243. This author places them in tenth century A. D. from a standpoint of its study of paleography and coincidence of time of Gaganasiva with tenth century A. D. in several sources of different places.

98. B. A. Saletor—Ancient Karnāṭaka Vol. I. pages 388-389.

99. Ed. U.S. Sharma—The Sarvadarśana Saṁgraha of Mādhavāchārya p. 320.

100. and 101. Ibid.

102. Ibid Someśvar temple Inscription of Ranipur Jharial also "Gaganaiksatvayaṁ Prabhuh Śivah"

103. and 104. Ibid. R. G. Bhandarkar Vaiṣṇavism, Śaivism and Minor Religious systems p. 124.

105. Ibid. p. 124. Ed. U. S. Sharma. The Sarvadarśanasamgraha of Mādhavāchārya. pp. 328-329.

106. Ed. U. S. Sharma—The sarvadarśanasaṁgraha of Mādhavāchārya p. 329.

107. Ibid. p. 329.

108. Ibid. p. 329.

109. Ibid. p. 329.

110. R. G. Bhandarkar—Vaiṣṇavism, Śaivism and Minor Religious systems pp. 124-125 Ed. U. S. Sharma—The Sarvadarśanasamgraha of Mādhavāchārya pp. 331-332.

111. Dr. S. N. Dasgupta—A history of Indian Philosophy Vol. V. p. 26.

112. R. G. Bhandarkar—Vaiṣṇavism, Śaivism and Minor Religious systems p. 125.

113. Ibid—p. 125.

114. Ed. U. S. Sharma—The Sarvadarśanasamgraha of Mādhavāchārya p. 323.

115. R. G. Bhandarkara—Vaiṣṇavism, Śaivism and Minor Religious systems p. 125.

116. Ed. U. S. Sharma—The Sarvadarśanasaṁgraha. p. 335.

117. Ibid—pp. 335-340.

118. Ibid—pp. 341-342.

119. Ibid—pp. 341-342.

120. Ibid—p. 341.

121. Ibid—p. 338.

122. R. G. Bhandarkar—Vaiṣṇavism Śaivism and Minor Religious systems p. 125.

123. Ibid—p. 125. Ed. U. S. Sharma—The Sarvadarśana Saṁgraha of Mādhavāchārya p. 338.

124. Ibid.

125. Ibid.

126. Ibid.

127. Ibid—p. 338-339, and 340.

128. Ibid

129. R. G. Bhandarkar—Vaiṣṇavism, Śaivism and Minor Religious systems p. 125. Ed. U. S. Sharma—The Sarvadarśana Saṁgraha of Mādhavāchārya. p. 336-337.

129A. Ibid.

130. Ibid.

131. Ed. U. S. Sharma—The Sarvadarśanasaṁgraha of Mādhavā chārya p. 334.

132. Ed. U. S. Sharma The Sarvadarśanasaṁgraha of Mādhavāchārya p. 334.

133. Ibid.

134.
and
135. Ibid—pp. 343-345.

136. Ibid—pp. 344-345.

137. Ibid—p. 344.

138. Ibid—pp. 344-345.

139. R. G. Bhandarkar—Vaiṣṇavism, Śaivism and Minor Religious systems. p. 124.

140. Epigraphia Indica Vol. XXI. pp. 148-149. In this Chandrehe Inscription of Prabodhaśiva the Mattamayūr Śaivāchārya are described as "Parihṛitāṇganāsangama".

WORSHIP OF FOLK-FORM OF 'LAXMI' IN ORISSA AND ITS SOCIO-CULTURAL ASPECTS

5

WORSHIP OF FOLK-FORM OF 'LAXMI' IN ORISSA AND ITS SOCIO-CULTURAL ASPECTS

Dr. U. N. Mohanty

It is rightly aaid that in the history of man no race possesses literature without folk literature. The folk songs and folk stories have no age. No one can say who are the people who composed them and ascertain how old they are. Existing folk beliefs, tales and customs are regarded as relics still surviving among backward races or in the less advanced sections of modern civilised communities.

Most societies have their own folk literature which reflects their beliefs and superstitions, their history and traditions and presents illuminating picture of their ways of like. Folklore continues to be a vital part of the life of the bulk of people. It contains the genesis of the tribe, the economic and institution pattern of the tribe, the economic and institution pattern of the tribe and the active and aesthetic exptession of the tribe. For understanding the social structure and culture of a tribe of community it is essential to know the myths, legends, tale proverbs and folk songs. The real value of folk literature as a source of socio cultural study lies not in its concern with particular person or incident but in its typical portrayal of situation, relationships and attitudes.

Like all other parts of this Indian sub-continent Orissa is rich in folklore. The history of Oriya folk literature is very old. The wondereful natural surroundings of Orissa made this literature a part and parcel of the lives of the Oriyas. Now this folk-literature received a set-back due to the impact of Modern civilisation and some of its essential features have undergone a great transformation.

A major part of Oriya folk stories were created on the basis of the Oriyas' worshipping to Gods and Goddesses There was no vedic or mythological basis behind those worship. In order to popularise it, story was made up for each and every worship. But when and by whom this system was introduced are not yet known. It is also very difficult to trace it. However this system of worship has been continuing for generations together. If we like we can take the local needs as its basis and origin in Orissa and all these worships are called as festivals of 'OSHA' or 'BRATA'.

Of all the Oshas in Orissa, 'DHĀNMĀNIKAS or 'GURUBĀRA OSHĀ' stands out. It is also known as 'Laxmī Pujā' the worship of Goddess Laxmī. But there is no similarity between this LAXMĪ PUJĀ and the mythological Laxmī worship. This puja stands as a symbol of Orissa's social and cultural glory. The Oriyas have tried to maintain peace and unity of the family and to get rid of caste-ridden social inequalities though it. A renonwned critic of Oriya literature. Dr. Rabindra Kumar Praharaj has rightly said that the significance behind the story of Laxmī Pujā is to get rid of untouchability from the society and it was Goddess Laxmi's demand before Lord Jagannāth that God dwells where there are holiness of conduct, sanctity of mind, sincereity in discharging one's duty, and where there is no discrimination on the basis of birth. All are equal before God, the creator. They should not be deprieved of their share of God's blessing. It will be a heinous if we do so.

In Indian mythology Laxmī the wife of Lord Vishṇu is worshipped as the Goddess of Wealth and beauty. We pray Her if we want peace, prosperity, happiness and Wealth Her image is considered to have all those benedictions. But in every home in Orissa we have MĀNABASĀ OṢHĀ which is a form of image worship of Laxmī. It is a kind of folk-form of the Goddess Laxmi. So it can not be denied that behind this ritual, there is a great tradition of Oriya's social and cultural life than his spiritual and devotional aspects and aspirations.

In ancient time the inhabitants of Orissa were mostly farmers. Paddy was their chief crop. The peace and prosperity or the sorrrows and sufferings of the Oriya family was linked with this crop. It was his greatest wealth. That is why every Oriya regarded paddy as Laxmī and looked upon it as a gift of divine grace.

Oriya farmer depends on nature for rain and starts cultivation in June. He harvests in the month of November, December ie., Margasira in Oriya. That is why this month is holy and pleasant for him When after long months of labour the farmer brings home paddy. The incarnation of Goddesses Laxmī his wife with an overshelming feeling of devotion arrenges the 'Dhanamanika Osha to welcome Her.

This festival or 'Oṣhā' is observed on every Thursday of Margasira. The farmer's wife makes a long preparation for it. Of course no image of metal or clay is needed for it. Paddy or Paddy-products are only used in it. Besides a small wooden stool and bambo-made basket are used in it. These two things, the farmer's wife keeps for years together. Before Margasira, a few stalls of paddy are collected and dried and kept carefully. Steps are taken to fill that aforesaid basket with new paddy and Bhoga (Offerings) Only white paddy is used in this Oshā.

From the very beginning of Mārgasira the wall and floor of the house are washed with cowdung. Different designs with watery pulp of new rice are drawn on floors and walls. These drawings are popularity known as JHUTI in Orissa. They are usually the handiworks of newly weded bride and young maidens at home. But other responsibilities of the festivals (Osha) are taken up by the housewife.

On every Thursday morning the housewife after finishing bath and other daily works builds the image. Then the image is placedon the wooden stool being decorated with the valuables ornaments and the bamboo basket full of paddy alongwith the paddy designs is kept by it. Different kinds of cakes made from new rice are offered to the Goddesses. No Oil Ghee is used in the preparation of these cakes. No priests or incantation (Mantras) is needed for this puja. Only the housewife completes the puja with full devotion. Of course the recitation of the Laxmipurana written by Oriya saint poet Balarama Das in 16th century has now been accepted as a tradition. From this puran we can get clear picture of folkstories connected to this Osha prevalent then.

The following is the thene of the story as described in the Laxmi purana.

Being permitted by Lord Jagannath, Goddess Laxmi went out on a round to the city. She happened to see immoral and irregular acts in the high caste families. She was pleased at the good manners of Sreeyā, a lowcaste woman dwelling at the far end of the village and blessed her. Śreeyās' small cottage was filled with riches and sandle-wood smell came out of it. Lord Balarām came to know it and persuaded Jagannāth to drive Laxmī out of the temple on the charge of her going to untouchable Śreeyā's house. Lord Jagannāth sent Laxmī away and she went to heaven (Vaikuṇṭhapur). But before her departure she cursed Jagannath that He and his brother would suffer poverty for twelve years and no rice, water and dress would be available to them.

Then Laxmī lived in a beautiful palace built by Viswakarmā

at her instance. She ordered the demons (Vetālas) to steal all the property from the temple. The temple lost its sanctity. The priests also left it. After two day's fasting Balarām and Jagannāth went round to quench hunger by begging. No body gave them alms. They were rather mocked at as unfortunate (Laxmichhadē). At last two brothers unknowingly arrived at Laxmī's residence. They begged for rice and vegetables to cook their food even if they knew from the female attendant (Dāsī) that it was a low-caste woman's house. But Laxmī played a trick upon them. The flame in the fireplace was reduced and water in the coocking pot did not get heated. Balarām broke the cooking pot out of disgust and proposed to dine at Laxmī's house. Laxmi prepared delicious dishes and staying at the background provided food to the brothers. She also sent burnt cake for the brothers at the end of their meal which they were habituated to eat with. This made the brothers to recollect Laxmī and they repented for their own deed. When Jagannath knew that this was Laxmī's house, he went in and begged excuse. Laxmī returned to the temple after getting assurance from the two brothers that there would be no discrimination between the lowcaste (Chaṇḍāl) and the high.caste (Brāhmin) in the Mahāprasād (Offering in the temple) of the temple.

The aforesaid story has two objectives (i) All irrespective of castes have equal right to worship the lord. and (ii) in domestic life woman has also equal right with man,

It is known that in ancient time Orissa had a caste ridden society thought there was no enough mythological basis for such caste descrimination. It was a brahmindominated society in which untouchables were segregated. This system continued till the end of the 19th century also. Those so-called untouchables were not allowed to enter into the temples. They did not even dare to worship gods and goddesses in their own houses. No other caste except the brahmins had a right to study the

'Sāstras' As the saint-poet Balarām Das was himself a non-brahmin he had to face a great ordeal to establish his right. To study 'Sāstras' in Oriya language was also considered a crime. In 15th century the Sudrapoet Saralā Dās had to write the 'Mahābhārata' in Oriya under the plea that is was God's dictate to him. The Oriya Bhāgabat by brahmin poet Jagannath Das was named 'Teli Bhagabat' and considered as an inferior book by the brāhmins. In order to get rid of all these social ills, the institution of Laxmīpujā was a novel attempt. It was because of this Laxmīpujā was petrormed by the rich as well as the poor irrespective of caste. This 'Oṣhā' worship also played a major role in establishing unity and brotherhood in the society. The presence of Laxmī in the house of the low caste woman and ultimate surrender of Jagannath to the will of Laxmi echo definitely a revolutionary step against untouchability in Oriya Laxmi purana.

In the past woman had no right in the family. She had to tolerate all injustice and oppression of man without protest. She was considered defenceless therefore she was deliberately meted out with oppresion. But the aforesaid story has shown that the peace and happiness in the family can be achieved only if man and woman exhibit mutual affection love and respect. Woman is considered to be the Laxmī of the house. If she is driven out, the family is ruined. So Lord Jagannāth himself said.

"I drove out my wife, a Laxmī incarnate, And we two brothers wander about. How unfortunate."

Besides all these the story throws light on some aspects of man and woman's daily life. At that time the villagers were ignorant of health care, as a result of which they suffered from deadly diseases. This knowledge was considered to be the commands of this holy scripture. Some of such instructions are :

A man who sleeps under the shadow of a cot, takes curd at night, shaves his face at a barber's house, splits rice on floor while eating or throws away excess rice being unable to eat, is deprived of the blessings of Goddess Laxmī and leads pathetic life.

In addition to fulfulling its social domestic and personal objectives this 'Oṣhā' has inspired the Oriya woman not only to keep her traditional care in tact, but to continue with and improve upon it. The excellence of art exhibited on the temples of Orissa is the greatest sign of the Oriya peoples' aesthetic sense. In the past all the houses in villages were made of mud. The walls and floors of these houses were being decorated with different design of JHUTI on the occasion of the 'DHĀNA-MĀNIKA OṢHĀ' This provided on opportunity to the newly married brides and unmarried maidens to exhibit the excellence of their artistic tallent secondly the walls were usually damaged and looked ugly in the rainy season. Their repair was badly needed so from the beginning of the month of Margasira November-December this repair was under taken and it was considered better to look after one's own house within a time limit. This 'Osha' provides opportunity for it.

It is because of the popularity of this 'Dhanmanika Osha' Balaram Das composed The Laxmi Purān a long narrative poem in the 16th century. After it a stong literary tradition in Oriya has been established on the basis of this book. Many Kāvyas and Plays have been written on it. Of course this Dhānmanika Osha has been given new dimension these days.

In western Orissa on the basis of this Osha atribal Community earned their lot in Trebal area. They are known as 'Devagonia' or Devaguru. They are called 'Bhaktas' They go round different places an recite the lines of the story of this 'Osha' They carry with them the image of Laxmī made of paddy and also other images. Their recitation is always aceompanied by a vina or musical instrument.

The glorious traditions of Orissa which lie behind there 'Vratas' and 'Oshas' will still come to limelight if the stories about those 'Oshas' are analysed more, Moreover we also come to know from these stories that the social and cultural life of the villages though ignorant and uncivilised was of high standard. Therefore these (Osha) and the stories about them deserve special studies.

KANDHAS AND GUNIVIDYA

6

KANDHAS AND GUNIVIDYA

Dr. Dolagobinda Bishi
Principal, P. S. College Saintala

In Tāntric practices miraculous power are attained. This miraculous power is Guṇīvidyā in Western Orissa. The miraculous practices were present in human culture even in the prehistoric age. These practices are the primary concepts of Tantra, although Tantra does not mean miraculous power alone. At present by Kandha Vidyā or Gaṇḍavidyā we believe the miraculous practices bases on Tāntric tradition. The Khandhas believe Gods, Goddess, Phantoms, spirits, and miraculous practices. When a Kandha suffers from diseases, meets an accident and falls into danger by the savage animal, he thinks that these misfortunes are caused due to the 'Super natural powers. In the Kandha village its remedy is done by the tantric practitioner called Guṇiān, Deheliā, Diārī, Jāni Jhānkar, Jhāru and Nāru. To the people of this class a simple Kandha respects out of fear. The Kandhas believe that the tantric practitioner called Guniān can be a tiger, a snake, a bull, a bear or any other savage animal, and can kill his enemies worshipping the Goddess of Mountain. They also believe that when man becomes deed, his soul moves else where independently. So, the Gunian who desires to harm his enemy, controlls the free spirit of a corpse. The person to die suffers according to the nature of 'Mantra' applied by him. To escape from a notorious Tāntrist the Kandha practice a saving device called 'Jiukita'.

It is not easier to be a Tāntrist or Gunian. It requires some preparation. practice and rituals. A Tantric teacher becomes necessary. The Tāntrist follows strong ruls for becoming eligible for these practices. In the primary stages the tantric practitioner does not cut his hair and nail, wear oil, flower and cosmetics, share the bed of a woman, touch the menstruated woman, sit on the beds of others, go to the unsacred place, and eat the cooked food of others. Without cutting his hair, he converses it into a matted lock. According to the Kandha's believe a child born with the matted lock of hair is eligible for becoming a Guniān by birth. A new comer to this field is directed to go to the cremation ground at night alone and is examined with various fear by his teacher. When the teacher is convinced that, his disciple is fearless he accepts him as his disciple and gives the 'Mantras' to practise. The disciple becomes free from fear going many times to the cremation ground and fearful places where white and black goats are sacrificed, buffalo is killed for Goddess worship, Sulia festival is instituted, Chhatardharnī is situated, and the prostitutes live. soils from these places are powdered on the body of the new disciple of Tantric practice. The disciple tries to bring a child from seven to eight month from the mother's womb. To be a best Gunian this becomes necessary but to be an ordinary Gunian this practice is not prescribed. Either from his own village or from the village of others the disciple brings the pregnant woman by his magical practices or by encharming or by showing any kind of pre-text. The pregnant women must have been healthy, free from wound or injury elder, and should be in the state of first conception. Such a woman is generally attracted by the Tāntric practice. This tāntric practice requires few eggs, the child of a hen, rice made from unboiled paddy, and mixed with haldi, Kalāsur (wine) ghugul, (scented materials created scent by fire) vermillion and collyrium and Mandār flower. With these materials the disciple proceeds with teacher at the midnight of a good day to the nearest of the house of the pregnant woman in tantric advices. If any bad symbol is seen, they stop their going and return home. They again try in another night which is considered good for that purpose. Arriving near the house of that woman, the teacher first ensures protection of his body and that of his disciple by his Mantra called Vajrakilaṇī. Then he makes unconscious all other members of the pregnant woman is family by a magic practice called 'Bhelkā-Jhumrā-Vāhan' By this mantra every body is made to sleep and the woman in need comes out of the home by the Mantra power even opening the door. She comes directly near the teacher and waits for his order. The hair on the head of that woman is made lose and the object called 'Chaunrī' is brought and given to the disciple by the teacher. This Chaunrī becomes useful at the time of Tāntric application. Both the teacher and disciple (Guru and Chelā) take her to a lonely place. The pregnant woman obeys by the charming power all the orders of the teacher. In the lonely place the teacher draws a tāntric diagram by giving soil ridge. The diagram is called 'yantra' and is especially the 'yantra' of Chāmuṇḍākāli, Humādumā and Venden. The women is asked to sleep over the diagram. After the sleeping of that women in an upward face, she is made necked and a Lāutumbā of needed shape is kept at the mouth of the generative organ of the woman. By the application of Mantra the abortion is caused. At the time of the application of 'Mantra' the disciple remains very careful to save the abortion falling the earth. The disciple preserves the oil and the clothes of the generative organ of the woman which comes to the work at the time of tāntric application. Such woman hardly survives after these type of tāntric action. After abortion the fleshy essence are cut into pieces and dried by a tantric process with the help of fire and smoke. Then all these pirces were kept in a new and unused earthern vessel. According to necessity one or two holes are made below the earthern vessel. The hole containing earthern vessel is kept above another earthern vessel which does not contain a hole. These two earthern vessels in the joint manner are kept above the third earthern vessel which remains full of water. With a tāntric mystification all these three earthern vessels are kept over a furnace causing fire from the below. Under the presure of the heat the fleshy essence discharges juice which through the hole of the first earthern vessel are deposited in the second earthern vesṣel. During this tāntric process Mantras are cited by the preceptor. Then the chopped head of an unmarried man is brought. This head is grinded into particles by the application of Mantra. These particles are mixed with the Juice obtain from the pressurisation of the fleshy essence or 'Garbhapiṇḍa'. This mixture is first adorned on the forehead of the disciple, then in all his limbs. Some of the mixture are drunk by the disciple with the water mixed with cowdung. Then the preceptor gives him a cane fitted with a brass hold at the top of the cane and accompanied by a picture of the head of a Tāntric goddess. He is also given a copper ring consecrated by Mantras. After doing all these things the disciple becomes a Tāntric of speech effication and at any time may assume the form of any animal according to his wishes. This Tantric process is known a 'Suanrasrasa' ordinary Gunians can not achieve this work. The ordinary Gunians get control over the Mantra pleasing a goddess like Masanichandi, of Kandha culture. The tantric deities of Kandha culture are suffixed as Muni, Suni, Kuni, and Khai. They are generally worshipped under trees like Semal, Dumer Mahul Phalsa, Rengal and Surni.

For the tantric practices the Anla tree is very favourable. The Kandhas believe that either at the Anla tree or its fruits the fantams, gobblins and bad spirits take their shelter. They may come to the floor at any moment they desire. The tantrist of the Kandha caste control the spirits within the fruits by his sub-ordination to rule and watching at the bottom of the tree. By bringing so many fruits of this nature by tantric process an oil is prepared from these fruits in the above sited process by the help of three earthern vessels. The juice of the fruits are obtained by this way. There after the chopped head of a girl who is especially dies before delivery at the stage of pregnancy or within the first seven days from the first menstruation is grinded to the particles. These particles are mixed with the fruit juice and an oil is prepared. This oil is known as 'Aenlātel' This oil is used on the body or head, it makes the tāntrist owner of uncommon tantric power. This oils is very useful at the time of tāntric practices. These are all secret knowledge and procedure. Its diagrams, Mantras, and Tāntric procedures are not published ordinarily, but the disciple learns it from the preceptor in an oral tradition. In Tāntric practices of the Kandhas no discrimination of male and female are made. Both the male and female are equally qualified for it. Of course the preceptor judges the eligibility of woman for the tantric practise by several tests. The female tantric practitioner keep lock of hair on the head. The female practitioner are most efficient than the male tantric practitioner. In Tāntric practices consecreted women become witch through hard tāntric rituals. The faith on witch-craft is found every where in Oḍishā a land of tantric culture. The people are affraid of the witch in Kandha village. Whenever a child or a teen ager dies of fever or anaemia or for other reason the Kandha suspects a female tantric practitioner as the cause of his/her death. There after he brings a faithful tāntrist or Diārī 'or' Jani or the village Jhāṇkar and expresses before him about his suspect. If any of this people either by Bharni or infusing the divine spirits and predicting thereby by standing the motion of air in the nostrils, the predictable calculation by chalk or by super natural paddy art acuses the female as witch then entire village unitedly torturethat woman by cutting nail and hair, by causing her bathe with the water mixed with cowdung or the water used by the swine and forcing her to drink that water. By doing this they believe that such action eliminates the witchly qualities from that woman. As punishment the two front teeth of her mouth are broken by beating and inserting human stools within it. If she cries in this then she is proved as innocent. If at all she is a real witch she is not puzzled by this. The Kandhas believe that the witches move in the midnight keeping lamps on the lower zaw and being nacked eats human stool, for this it is, proved by inserting human stool whether she is witch or not. Kandhas believe that, the witch cries if biten with the branches of 'Jadā' and Tharthari tree She becomes chided when salt is given on the reverse of a leaf, if the finger is indicated towards the mountain and if the nose is rubbed in her front. The Kandhas examine by all these methods whether a woman is a witch or not. It is believed that the look of the witch causes harm to the children. To face a witch at the mid night is very dangerous. Proficient Gunians can do it. They do not arrive the witch from the front side. Having protected their body by a Vajrakilā Mantra they hide themself at the place of the moving of the witches. When the witches being nacked, eat human stools, their clothes or sari are taken away by the Guniān, with courage. Having applied Mantras on these clothes, they control the witches, their works or at the time of necessity eliminates her witchly quality. In elimination of the wicthly quality that cloth is inserted into the wooden container where the swaine drinks water by Tantric process called 'Astakilāchāpen' witch craft is a dengerous practice. The Kandhas believe that the witch can do every thing they like. The witch in Kandhan language (The language of Kandha) is called Tanchi Chuhinī Sursuri, and Bhirvimi.

According to their believe the witch can kill any body when she desire by sucking the blood. The witch goes to the house of any man at the midnight in an invisiable way and climbs to the roof and sucks the blood of any man and woman of that house by inserting a thread-through a hole and taking the help of the thread as a pipe. After few days, the victim dies of anuemic fever. The witches kill not only the man but also the domestic animals by this method. The Kandhas believe that, the Guniās and the witches cause many harm to the people by this tāntric practice. When the become angry with any body, they substitude the bones of the fish. The bones of the snake, the covers of the egg, sainds small stones, the nutsof Haldi and the seeds of Turmolive tree as also the carbon are inserted taking away the bones of the victims. This is knows as 'Pesen' or 'Nāsen' When anexpert tantrist is invited for protection, he enables the victims to live from death having broughtout the materials inserted by the witch or Gunian. This process is knows as 'Ulṭen' or returing the evil power towards the witch or gunian. An expert gunian can cause a return of the evil and fatal influence of another gunian by the tantric power of returning. If the return fatal force is not tolerated by the applier of that force then he either dies or becomes the victim of fatal diseases. When ever a tantrist sends his force for harm, he takes a tree as a symbol of the victim or an image made of wood, cloth, Haldi and a forest grass called Vave or an image made of the Kusha grass as the symbol of the victim. The force applied so, attacks the Victim and in absence of any tāntric protection kills him. This killing procedure is similar to the 'black-magic' of other premitive class of the world. The Kandhas call it 'Pāngan' and 'Nasan'. The Gunians generally worship Bhairon, Chamenkālī, Maśānkālī. Dhumenkālī, Dāṇgua, Suliā, Kālisundrī, Humādumā, Vīr, Sātvhanī, Gods and Goddesses of the 'Muni and Suni class along with their family deity called 'Pidar'. By the charming power they apply the power of encharming the young girls and woman prepare charming amulets, Collyrium, mirror. comb, scents and flowers having retualised it by 'Mantras'. In this circumstance the gunians worship Vinkei, Humādumā, Joldhāngri, Panken, Suliā, Chakardhar, and Venden, in tāntric procedure. To encharm they require the inner threads and clothes of the maiden young woman or married woman of the time of menstruation, their hair dressing thread, water of the bathing place, dust of the feets and bathing Haldi. The enchanting are of many type. They are knows as Rajmuhunī, Jalkāmuhunī, Thakthakamuhunī, Lakhlakha muhunī, charchara muhunī, Getha muhunī, Dhundri muhunī, and Bhelka muhunī etc. The tantrists can control by enchanting the fantoms, spirits even divine powers, tigers, snakes and other power of the earth. They can also save the life and property of man from the evil spirits and wild animals through the process of Dehakilā, Gharkilā, Khetkilā, and Khatqkilā and by making amnilet, disc, protective materials called Kabacha and confining the evil spirits by powerful mantras. They get rid of various diseases like cholera and small pox by this tantric practice. According to their believe all the goddesses are the deities of several diseases. They are subject to the prayer of Gunian, Jani, and Jhankar. The Gunians apply the method of Bharen, Nāchen, Vakten, Ulgan, Jagen, and Valen in tāntric process for the removing diseases. Though the Kandha people have a physician called Damrā the gunians also give medicines of such types. Having adopted tantric practices they prepare medicines. The Kandhas believe that the Guniāns or tāntrists may talk directly with these super natural spirits. It is a common duty and a profession of the Gunians to cure diseases, to remove bad vision and neutralise the poison of snake bite and other poisons.

Gradually the Kandhas are loosing their traditional practices by the pressure and the faith with the light of civilisation. Changes of believes, practices and others have discouraged their tāntric practices. The Tantric practice Muiṭhmara (competition with Tantric powers among the tantrists) has disappeared almost. Now, all their secret practices of Sadhana are subject of deep research only. All these facts in this essay are collected from the saying of old Guniāns of Kalahandi district and Kandhān tract.

Dr. Dolagovinda Bishi
Principal
P. S. College, Saintala

BIBLIOGRAPHY

BIBLIOGRAPHY

Name of the work (a) Literary texts and translations—(Indian)	Name of the Author/Editor/ Translator / Publisher / Place and year of Publication,
1. Aṣṭasāhasrikā Prajñā-pāramitā.	Ed. R. L. Mitra, A. S. B. Calcutta 1888.
2. Ārya Mañjusri Mūla-kalpa Vol-I (1920) Vol-II (1921), Vol-III (1925).	Ed. T. G. Sastri, Ananta Sayana Grantravali Triven-drum (1920-1925).
3. Advayasiddhi—The Tān-tric View of Lakṣmīṅkarā.	Dr. R. P. Mishra, Kant Pub-lications Delhi 1995.
4. Brahma Nirupaṇa Gītā.	Bhima Bhoi, Dharma Gran-tha Store Cuttack 1981.
5. Bhāgavata Purāṇa.	Tr. J. M. Sanyal, Calcutta 1952.
6. Bauddhagān O Dohā.	Ed. Mr. H. P. Sastri, B. S. P. Calcutta Bangabda—1358.
7. Bodhāyana Dharma Sūtra.	Ed. E. Hultzch, London 1884.
8. Chaitanya Charitāmṛita.	A. K. Ghosh, H. N. Press Cuttack 1929.
9. Charyāgītikoṣa.	Dr. P. C. Bagchi and Santi Bhiksu Sastri Visvabharati Calcutta 1956.

Name of the work (a) Literary texts and translations—(Indian)	Name of the Author/Editor/ Translator / Publisher / Place and year of Publication.
10. Dhvanyāloka of Ānanda-varddhan.	Motilal Banarsidass New Delhi 1935.
11. Ekāmra Purāṇa.	L. Garavadu, Cuttack 1933.
12. Gautama Dharma Sūtra.	L. Srinivasacharya, Mysore 1917.
13. Gautamīya Tantra.	Ed. B. Jha, C. S. S. Baranasi Vikrama Samvat 2033 (1977).
14. Gītagovinda.	Jayadeva, Dharmagrantha Store Cuttack 1950.
15. Hevajra Tantra.	D. L. Snellgrove, Oxford University 1959.
16. Haṭhayoga Pradīpikā.	S. Yogindra, Bombay Sakabda 1874.
17. Iśvara Pratyabhijñā of Utpala Deva.	Com. A. Gupta, Srinagar 1918.
18. Jñānasiddhi of Indrabhūti.	Ed. B. Bhattacharya, in Two Vajrayana Works G. O. S. Baroda 1929.
19. Kālikā Purāṇa.	Bombay Samvat 1964.
20. Kṛitya Ratnakara.	A. S. B. Calcutta 1925.
21. Kāmakalāvilāsa.	Ed. P. Nath, Madras 1961.

Name of the work (a) Literary texts and translations—(Indian)	Name of the Author/Editor/ Translator / Publisher / Place and year of Publication.
22. Lakṣhmī purāṇa.	Balaram Das, Berhampur 1960.
23. Matsya Purāṇa.	Ed. H. N. Apte, A. S. S. Poona 1907.
24. Nyāyakoṣa.	B. Jhalakikar, B. R. I. Poona 1928.
25. Nārada Purāṇa.	Bombay Sakabda 1848.
26. Rudrayāmala Tantra	R. C. Kak, Kashmir 1941.
27. Saddharma Puṇḍarīka Sūtram.	Ed. P. L. Vaidya, Mithila Institute Darbhanga 1960.
28. Sekoddeśaṭikā of Nāḍapāda.	M. E. Karelli, G. O. S. Baroda 1941.
29. Suvarnaprabhāsa Sūtram.	Ed. Dr. S. Bagchi Darbhanga 1967.
30. Śrīguhyasamāja Tantra.	Ed. Dr. S. Bagchi, Darbhanga 1965.
31. Sarvadarśanasaṁgraha of Mādhvāchārya.	Ed. U. S. Sharma, C. S. S. Baranasi 1964.
32. Sāralā Mahābhārata (Oriya).	Dharmagranta Store Cuttack 1970.
33. Yoginī Tantra.	Pt. K. L. Mishra, Bombay Samvat 2013.

Name of the work (b) Literary texts and translations (Non-Indian).	Name of the Author/Editor/ Translator / Publisher / Place and year of Publication.
1. Ancient India as described by Ptolemy.	J. W. Me. Crindle, Calcutta 1885.
2. Contribution a la bibliographic du kanjuret du Tanjur-les texts boudhiques au temps du Roi khri-sron-ldebcan.	M. La Lou, Paris 1953.
3. Die Geschichte der Dalai Lamas.	G. Schulemann, Heidelburg 1911.
4. Eine Tochter Tibets, Leben im Land der Vertriebenen Gotter.	R. D. Taring, Hamburg 1972.
5. Introduction a' l' histoire du Tibet.	J. Bacot Paris 1962.
6. L'enseignement Vimalakirti—(Vimalakirtinirdesa).	E. Lamotte Louvain 1962.

Secondary Sources

Name of the work	Name of the Author/Editor/ Translator / Publisher / Place and year of Publscation.
(b) Literary texts and translations (Non-Indian).	
1. A History of Indian Literature Vol-I and Vol-II.	Dr. M. Winternitz New Delhi 1972.
2. Ancient Geography of India.	A.Cunningham Calcutta,1924.
3. Ancient Indian Folk Cults.	V. S. Agrawal Varanasi, 1965.
4. An Introduction to Buddhist Esoterism.	Dr. B. Bhattacharya, C. S. S. Baranasi 1964.
5. An Introduction to Tāntric Buddhism.	Dr. S. B. Dasgupta University of Calcutta, 1974.
6. A History of Indian Philosophy Vol-I, II and V.	Motilal Banarsidass Delhi—1975.
7. Archaeological Remains at Bhubaneśvar.	Dr. K. C. Panigrahi, Kitab Mahal Cuttack 1981.
8. Buddhism in Drissa.	Dr. N. K. Sahu, Utkal University 1958.
9. Buddhist Art in India, Ceylon and Javā.	J. P. Vogel Clarendon Press Oxford 1936.
10. Comparative and Critical study of Mantraśāstra.	M. B. Jhavery, Ahmedabad 1944.

Name of the work (b) Literary texts and translations (Non-Indlan).	Name of the Author/ Editor/ Translator / Publisher / Place and year of Publication.
11. Cultural Profiles of South Kośala.	J. P. Singhdeo Delhi 1987.
12. Development of Hindu iconography.	J. N. Banerjee, Calcutta University 1956.
13. Encyclopaedia of Religion and Ethics.	J. Hastings Edinburg 1915.
14. Erotic Art of the East.	Philip Rawson London 1973.
15. Fragments of Indian Culture.	Dr. R. P. Mishra Punthi Pustak Calcutta 1995.
16. Glory of the Divine Mother Devī Māhātmya.	S. Sankaranarayan Madras 1968.
17. History of Drissa Vol—I and—II.	R. D. Bannerjee Delhi 1980.
18. History of Beṅgali literature.	Dr. S. Sen, Sahitya Academy New Delhi 1962.
19. History of Orissa Vol—I.	Dr. H. K. Mahtab Cuttack 1959.
20. Indian Philosophy Vol-I.	S. Radhakrishnan George Allen and Unwin Ltd London (1923-1977).

Name of the work (b) Literary texts and translations (Non-Indian).	Name of the Author/Editor/ Translator / Publisher / Place and year of Publication.
21. Jagannāth in History and Religious Traditions of Orissa.	Dr. G. Mahapatra, Punthi Pustak Calcurta 1982.
22. Kashmir Śaivism Part—I.	J.C. Chatterjee, Srinagar 1914.
23. Kulārṇava Tantra (In Hindi) Ed. Pandit R. Sukla.	Kalyana Mandir Prakashan Prayag 1980.
24. Kandhajātira Vivāha Prathā (In Oriya).	Dr. D. Bishi, Publisher D. P. Sharma, Chhan Chchhada Saintala 1990.
25. Kośala Vaktṛitāmālā.	D. A. V. College Titilagarh 1977.
26. Mystic Tales of Lama Tārānāth.	B. N. Dutta Calcutta 1944.
27. Neo Upaniṣadas.	A. D. Pusalkar Bharatiya Vidya Bhavan Bombay 1954.
28. Origin of Jagannāth Deity.	J. P. Singhdeo, Gian Publishing House Delhi 1991.
29. Purāna Tattva Vimarśa.	K. Tripathy Lucknow 1961.

	Name of the work	Name of the Author/ Editor/ Translator / Publisher / Place and year of Publication.
(b)	Literary texts and translations (Non-Indian).	
30.	Rise and Fall of the Śailodbhavas.	Dr. S. C. Behera, Punthi Pustak Calcutta 1982.
31.	Sidelights on the History and Culture of Orissa.	Dr. M. N. Das, Vidyapuri Cuttack 1977.
32.	SAHAJAYĀNA—A Study of Tāntric Buddhism.	Dr. R. P. Mishra, Punthi Pustak Calcutta 1991.
33.	Tantrayāna Art.	S. K. Saraswati, A. S. B. Calcutta 1967.
34.	Tantra, the Indian Cult of Ecstasy.	Philip Rawson, Vikas Publishing House Pvt. Ltd. Delhi-6 1974.
35.	The Divine Master-Life and Teachings of Guru Nānakdev.	S. Singh, Gian Publishing House Delhi 1989.
36.	The Religions of Hindus.	K. W. Morgan, New York 1953.
37.	The Śaktas.	E. A. Payne, Oxford University Press 1933.
38.	Śrī Jagannāth and Nepal.	A. Das and S. R. Sarma, Vidyapuri Cuttack 1986.

Name of the work	Name of the Author/Editor/
(b) Literary texts and translations (Non-Indian).	Translator / Publisher / Place and year of Publication.
39. Lord Jagannāth—the Microcosm of Indian spiritual Culture.	S. Mahanty Bhubanesvar 1982.
40. The Cult of Jagannāth.	Dr. K. C. Mishra Calcutta 1971.
41. Vīravikrama Nāṭakāvalī.	Ed. Dr. U. N. Mahanty, Bharati Press Titilagarh.
42. Viplavī Kavi Sāralā Dās.	Ed. Dr. U. N. Mahanty, D. A. V. College Titilagarh 1985.

INDEX

INDEX

ERRATA

Page	*Line*	*Printing mistake*	*Correct reading*
3	7	creaters	creators
5	12	Ade	Ado
5	13	durhane	durhano
6	1	testimenies	testimonies
6	3	legshaped	logshaped
6	27	inscriptions	inscription
7	27	Purusettama	Purusottama
8	6	neeks and corners	nooks and corners of the world
9	28	knows	known
9	31	suggests	suggest
10	19	phenomena	phenomenon
10	30	Sectarian	sectarian
10	34	not to have	not to hate
13	15	corner	corners
13	21	vyomasiva-I	Vyomaśiva-I
14	4	Caste	caste
14	13	paramaśiva	Paramaśiva
14	15	Sevete	Sevate
14	33	cult the	cult, the
15	20	vaitāla	Vaitāla
15	21	her the	here the
16	1	Nidravati	Nidrāvatī
16	30	grave	grace
17	9	Divya	divya
17	15	teaches man	teaches, man
21	15	All her religious	All her religions
22	6	was much more greater	were much greater
23	21	majestice	majestic

Page	*Line*	*Printing mistake*	*Correct reading*
24	17	Ie ; puri	i. e. Puri
24	30	ideologies doctrines	ideologies, doctrines
25	11	oustom	out come
25	23	tenincarnations	ten incarnations
26	25	representin Sakta element	representing Sakta elements
26	27	Jagannath Balabhadra	Jagannath, Balabhadra
27	3	Jagannathtriad	Jagannath-triad
27	6	vaisnative	vaisnavite
27	24	Vaisna king	Vaisnava king
27	26	Hi with	Him with
28	1	he founder	the founder
28	6	an conclusively	and conclusively
28	11	This in now	This is how that
28	15	castes creeds	castes and creeds
29	1	The story in short is once	The story in short is that once
29	4	belongs	belonged
29	4-5	untouchables was	untouchables and was
29	26	high nor low	high or low
29	27	stody	story
29	33	brahmin	Brahmin
30	8	pat	past
30	10	swallen	swellen
30	12	of carry out	to carry out
30	17	amon	among
30	. 6	stody	story
30	29	Governmen	Government
30	33	no allowed	not allowed
31	29	This is how the	This is how that
31	31	Uniting making	Uniting mankind
32	31	Sarara	Saralā
35	9	Union on	Union of

Page	Line	Printing mistake	Correct reading
35	11	Tāntra	Tantra
35	19	As far few	As few
39	20	As anga simply	Asanga simply
40	10	Mahāyān-ist	Mahāyānist
40	11	syste matised	systematised
40	17	Pāramitāna	Pāramitānaya
41	2	as tendency	as Cendency
41	8	Weitten	Written
41	9-10	Tathagatagujyaka	Tathagataguhyaka
41	18	new system	new system."
42	29	suggest	suggests
42	31	monaslery	monastery
43	31	organised in	organised into
44	27	motherl and	mother land
45	1	Bebgal	Bengal
45	2	in errogation	interrogation
46	7	Chwann	Chwang
48	4-5	Lanke śvari	Lanke-śvari
49	3	Saha Jasiddha	Sahajasiddha
49	5	a100 king	a king 100
49	25	Lakshmīkarā	Lakṣhmīṅkarā
50	14	Places	Plates
51	16	inscription	inscriptions
52	22	leaant	learnt
52	23	Padma Vajra	Padma vajra
53	25	Jnanga Vajra	Anaṅga Vajra
53	34	Kind	King
54	33	Rāhula ruchi	Rāhularuchi
54	34	Rāhul aruchi	Rāhularuchi
54	35	Rāhul abhadra	Rahulabhadra
55	9	Sahajasiddas	Sahajasiddhas
55	10	Virupā	Virupā
55	10	Kanhupāda	Kanhupāda
56	8-9	Some śvaradeva	Some-śvaradeva

Page	*Line*	*Printing mistake*	*Correct reading*
56	11	an	and
56	14	padmasambhava	Padmasambhava
67	12	Indian Saints	Indian saints
68	11	a all pervasive	an all-pervasive
69	17	Chacteri stics	Characteristics
69	33	Puritantic	Puritanic
70	3	pervesive	pervasive
70	16	Bhaki	Bhakti
70	23	throuth	through
71	15	Guru of Sikha	Guru of Sikhs
71	17	Comlpiled	Compiled
72	4	Integration	integration
72	4	the back ground	the background of
72	16	granta	grantha
73	12	Gita Govinga	Gita Govinda
73	19	has	his
75	31	Sikirs	Zikirs
77	28	rhythem	rhythm
80	1	Sadus	Sadhus
80	16	Nother	Northern
80	17	Southers	Southern
82	1	Jagyan	yajna
82	3	Jagyan	yajna
82	5	specially	Specially
82	6	palgun	phalguna
82	8	Jagyan	yajna
82	10	do	do
82	12	do	do
82	16	do	do
82	20	cheld	child
82	25-26	ammal gamation	amalgamation
103	23-24	other Saivite text[5] The Siddhanta doctrine	other Saivite text, [5] the Siddhanta doctrine

Page	*Line*	*Printing mistake*	*Correct reading*
104	3	bn	by
108	2	in Vayaviya	In vayaviya
108	30	delineatin	delineating
109	1	keeping	Keeping
110	18	mony places	many places
111	26-27	Sankhamathi **kādhipati**	Sankhamathikadhipati
113	1	Orisa	Orissa
113	3	Ahichtraka	Ahichhatraka
114	12	Mattamayura, Saiva	Mattamayura Saiva
114	16	Amarddha	Amarddā
114	20 and 22	Mattamayuranth	Mattamayūranāth
116	32	prefix of suffix	prefix or suffix
117	7	nor be can be	nor he can be
119	6-7	come of	came to
119	27	a number petty	a number of petty
120	1	indispensable	indispensably
121	9	choulder	shoulder
122	29	iadicated	indicated
128	28	Asamatakalusa	Asamāptakaluṣa
129	4	unquestionable Astavidyesvara	unquestionable status of Aṣṭavidyeśvara
129	21	paśas	pāśas
131	3	paramasive	Paramaśiva
132	3	Liberal	liberal
143	1	aaid	said
153	15	tantric	Tantric

PLATE I

Asta Mahabhaya Tara From Ratnagiri,
Patna Museum

PLATE II

Heruka, Ratnagiri.

PLATE III

Four Armed Jatamukta Avalokiteswara from Udayagiri Solapuama Temple of Cuttack.

PLATE IV

Padmapani Avalokiteswara from Khadipada, Orissa State Museum, Bhubaneswar.

PLATE V

Vajrasattva from Solampur, Indian Museum, Calcutta.

PLATE VI

Marichi, Ayodhya.

PLATE VII

The Image of Ekpāda Bhairava Ghodar Bhainro Dungrī

PLATE VIII

Śiva in meditative posture Ghodar

PLATE IX

Some Śvara Śiva Temple, Ranipur-Jharial

PLATE XII

Yoginī temple Ranipur-Jharial (Inner view)